SWEDISH CROSS-CUT

A canal passengerboat moored beside Vadstena Castle during a mid-way halt on the Göta Canal Journey.

SWEDISH CROSS CUT

A Book on the Göta Canal

BY ERIC DE MARÉ

Photographs by Eric de Maré and Erik Liljeroth

ALLHEMS FÖRLAG MALMÖ

These pictures show the harbours at either end of the Göta Canal—Stockholm and Gothenburg. LEFT, *the berth for canal boats in Stockholm is at Riddarholm Quay in the heart of the city.* ABOVE, *Gothenburg Harbour, one of the largest in Scandinavia. Passengers usually start their trip up the canal from here.*

INTRODUCTION

This book is about one of Europe's major navigations—Sweden's charming Blue Ribbon which crosses the country from its main port, Gothenburg, on the west to its capital, Stockholm, on the east. But, as its title indicates, the guide is intended to be more than a description of the Göta Canal route itself. It is a guide to Sweden-as-seen-from-the-waterway so that voyagers along it, whether travelling in their own craft or in one of the passenger steamers, may understand from the part something of the whole.

The book will therefore digress now and then. A timber bell-tower will provide the excuse for saying something about Swedish bell-towers in

general and about the peasant culture which produced them. An old castle will allow us to travel back in time. A timber farmstead, glowing in the bright evening sunshine, will give an opportunity as we glide along to digress on a Swedish speciality—the red protective paint from Falun which gives so much to the character of the Swedish landscape.

I have explored the waterway thoroughly and piecemeal—by canoe, motorboat, steamer and by towpath walks. The book will therefore reveal more about the places along the waterway than the traveller will himself be able to observe from the steamer's deck or during the brief periods when he can step on land during his journey of two-and-half days. For example, when crossing Lake Boren, you may glimpse several church spires topping the pine trees far off on the shore. What do the buildings really look like close-up? Do they hold any beautiful or significant monuments or paintings? I will tell you if they do and I will show you photographs. In that way perhaps I shall be able to satisfy your curiosity and to make your journey more interesting and enjoyable. You will probably be lying in your bunk along some parts of the route and then the book will keep watch for you so that you will at least hear about things of interest you have passed while sleeping.

I will also tell you about the fascinating history of the canal's building in which a great British engineer was involved. I will tell you, too, a little about the country as a whole, and about the two terminal towns of the journey. Dr. Ingvar Andersson has contributed a concise history of the country to give you your bearings in time. Thus the book may serve as a useful holiday companion and perhaps afterwards also as a souvenir of what, I trust, will have been a happy and memorable journey through one of the most romantic yet civilized countries of the world.

ERIC de MARÉ

London, June 1964

LEFT, *an old schooner on the cross-country waterway which exists primarily for commercial traffic. A considerable number of vessels pass through each year and the shipping is becoming more and more modern. The days of the sailing ships are numbered.*

CONTENTS

The Göta River is a comparatively wide waterway. (Photo by ERIC DE MARÉ.)

THE BACKGROUND

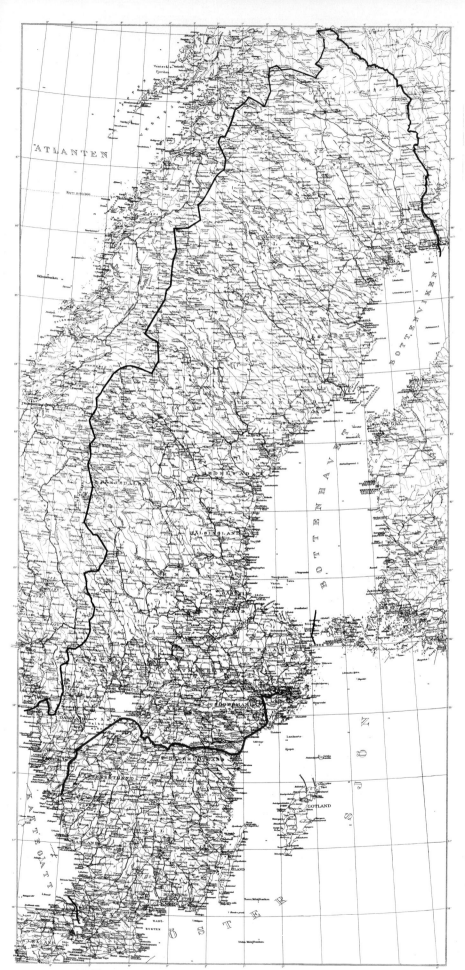

*Map of Sweden. The
Canal route from Go-
thenburg to Stockholm
marked in red.*

THE PREVIOUS PAGE,
RIGHT, *the rune stone
at Ledberg Church,
Östergötland, has an
armoured Viking
among its inscriptions.*

LEFT, *Sweden abounds
in beautiful medieval
churches. Many of
them, such as Rogslösa
in Östergötland, are
within reach of the
tourists on the Göta
Canal. Rogslösa is
famous for its ornate
door, dating from the
twelfth century.*

PLACE AND PEOPLE

THE CHARACTER OF THE COUNTRY

First let us examine the setting of the Göta Canal—the country itself. In several ways Sweden is physically strange. For one thing it is three times as long as it is broad; from top to bottom it measures 978 miles, a distance equal to that between the most southernly point of Sweden and Naples. North and south are quite different; the far north is the barren land of the wandering Lapps, mainly flat tundra country but bearing a massif to the west. Up there in the north two mountains rise among the others called Kirunavaara and Gällivare malmberg which are composed almost entirely of rich iron ore and provide a major source of Sweden's wealth. Below the north-western massif the mountains keep fairly close to the Norwegian frontier and from them the rivers run in a south-eastward direction towards the Baltic Sea. This is a useful gift of nature because the rivers melt first at their mouths and thus form valuable means of floating the timbers of the great forests down to the sawmills, the pulp mills and the ports. Timber is Sweden's second main source of wealth and is obtained from the endless forests of spruce and pine which cover more than half the country.

Apart from the mountains of the north, the land, though knolly, is comparatively flat. The south, mainly composed of the provinces of Skåne (Scania) and Blekinge is rather flat, being an extension of the Central European Plain. This is the country's granary and is more Danish in character than Swedish; indeed, it formed part of Denmark until the Peace of Roskilde in 1658 established Sweden's natural boundaries.

Separating the midlands and the southern plain is the rather barren, hilly country of Småland and Halland, which acted as a military buffer between Danes and Swedes in past times of warfare. These parts have produced the hardest breed of Swede, the Scotsmen of the country.

Above the southern plain the whole country is spattered with lakes of which there are no less than 96,000, large and small, covering a tenth part of the whole land. The area most closely covered with lakes lies between the

15

forest lands above the centre of the country and the southern plain. This part, which includes the ancient provinces of Östergötland and Västergötland, is both the Midlands and the Lake District of Sweden, the most interesting, the most historical and the most thickly populated part of the country containing the capital, the main port of Gothenburg, most of the larger industrial towns and the three largest lakes—Vänern, Vättern and Mälaren. In this area the landscape is fairly typical with its pine, birch and rowan trees, its lakes and its outcrops and ridges of gneiss and granite worn smooth by the glaciers as they retreated northwards thousands of years ago. Between the woods and the rocks lie the small undulating fields of the peasant farmers, here and there a small, trim town, a white church tower or a red timber farmstead, never far from some calm, blue lake or fjord. Right across this typical landscape runs the famous waterway which is the subject of this book.

In spite of the general style of the Swedish landscape, regions have their marked differences. The west coast, for instance, is unlike the east coast, although both have their extensive archipelagos. Indentations are deeper on the east than on the west and that geographical fact has affected history; it encouraged the Swedes in the past to expand eastward across the Baltic and south-eastward rather than westward because the east coast provided harbours with better natural protection than those of the west. Stockholm itself was founded as a port easily protected against marauders. The west coast is more bleak than the east with fewer trees and its skerries are often smooth and barren rocks. Both coasts, however, provide ideal yachting waters, especially so the tideless waters of the Baltic which include the lovely labyrinth of the Stockholm archipelago with its ten thousand isles.

The twenty-four provinces have each their own character, traditions and dialects, like the English counties, though today these provinces do not always coincide with the twenty-four modern administrative districts called *län*. In everyday speech, however, people still refer to the old cultural areas rather than to these *län*. Centuries ago when the old provinces were named, Sweden was roughly divided into three parts—Götaland, the land of the Goths, in the south; Norrland in the north; Svealand, the land of the Svear, Suoines or Swedes, in between. Our waterway runs mainly through Götaland—that is Västergötland on the west and Östergötland on the east.

HOW THE SWEDES LIVE

What of the Swedes today and their economy? The population is about seven and a half million, of which a million or so live in and around Stockholm. The area of the country is nearly twice that of England and it is thus among the most sparsely populated countries of Europe. Contrary to general

Cornfields in Skåne, the most southerly province and the granary of Sweden.

The population of Sweden is now about 7½ million, and more than half lives in towns. The standard of living is one of the highest in the world. By race and origin the Swedes are not as "pure" as is often asserted. In the course of time alien peoples have settled in Sweden.

RIGHT, Sweden's national wealth consists of iron and timber. The picture shows part of the mineral railway on the extensive Kirunavaara-Luossavaara orefields. The orefields can be seen in the background.

LEFT, Swedish timber is produced mostly in Norrland but lately a number of pulpmills have been started in central and southern Sweden. This picture shows a section of the timber industries at Holmsund near Umeå in the province of Västerbotten.

The vast tracts of Norrland are only very sparsely cultivated but forestry thrives. The picture shows a view of the province of Härjedalen.

foreign belief, not every Swede is tall, fair, blue-eyed and handsome, though the type is common enough; the race is by no means as "pure" as is commonly thought because Finns, Dutchmen, French Huguenots, Germans, Balts, Jews and Scots have settled in the country at different times and have intermarried with the descendants of those aboriginal stone-age settlers who followed the retreating glaciers northwards from Germania several thousand years ago. The author of this book is a typically untypical Swede being a British subject born in London of a mother from Gothenburg having a good deal of Scottish blood and a father from Dalarna with French Huguenot ancestors.

How do the Swedes live? Less than a century ago Sweden was a comparatively poor agricultural country but today, thanks to the intelligent exploitation of her water power and her basic raw materials of iron ore and timber, she is a rich industrial nation. This change of life has been achieved without creating the squalor and social unrest which have been the common results of rapid industrialisation and urbanisation in other countries. In 1800 the rural population was 85 per cent. of the whole; today it is only 20 per cent. In spite of that Sweden produces nearly all her own food from the nine per cent. of the surface of her land which can be farmed. Most of the farms are small peasant holdings supported by co-operative marketing organizations. Industries are immensely varied and include ship-building, heavy engineering, textiles, paper, matches, shoes, motorcars, ack-ack guns and nearly everything else you can think of. Timber and wood pulp are, of course, of the greatest importance, especially for exporting. Industry is mainly under private enterprise, though the State and the co-operatives own many works and public utilities. Tobacco and alcohol are state monopolies and the State owns one-third of the electric supply plant, some iron and steel works and the major part of the forests. Possessing hardly any coal and no oil of her own, Sweden relies for power on her White Coal, the hydro-electricity from her many water-falls. Now she is beginning to develop atomic power in order to become independent of the vagaries of rainfall and therefore of water power.

NEXT PAGE, ON THE LEFT, *Sweden is famous for her highly developed steel industry. The products made at the ball-bearing factory in Gothenburg (SKF) are exported all over the world.*—THE VIGNETTE ON THE RIGHT, *Viking helmets of the kind used during the Viking expeditions to England have been found on Swedish territory. This helmet comes from the province of Uppland.*

SWEDEN'S HISTORY

BY INGVAR ANDERSSON

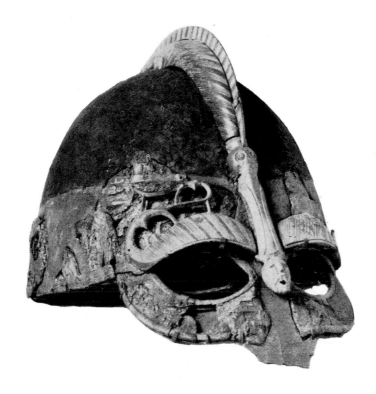

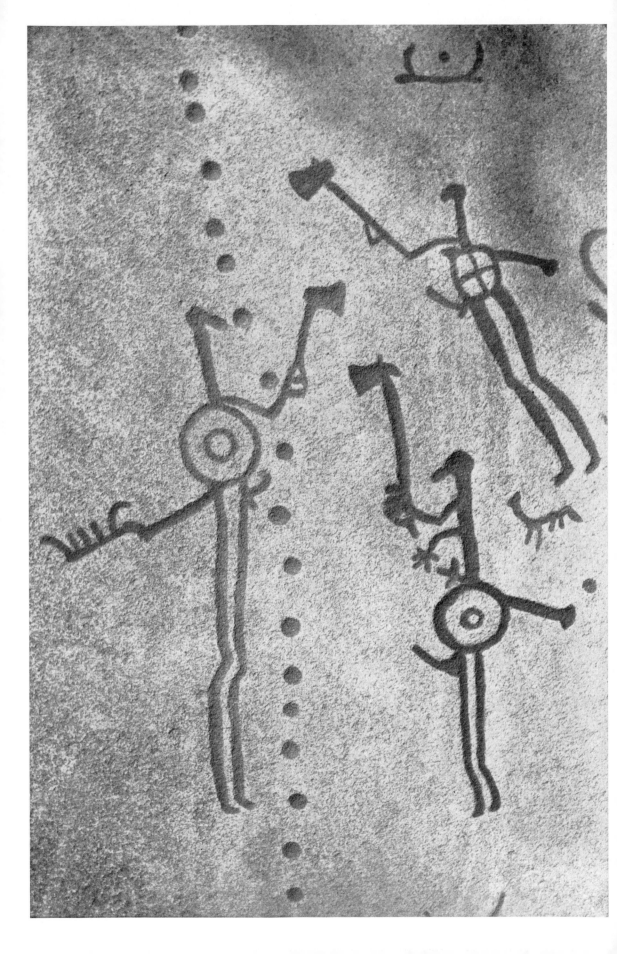

On the south coast of Sweden at Kåseberga stands one of the most impressive ancient monuments in the country: a stone ship, 67 metres long. It dates from the days of the Vikings.

Eons ago all of Sweden was covered by an incredibly thick ice cap. Fourteen thousand years have passed since it began to melt away in the southern parts, and about twelve thousand years ago the first primitive hunters began to follow the receding ice. Swedish geologists have made an intensive study of the annual, stratified deposits of clay left by the ice and have developed a dependable geochronic system. Thus we now know that the southernmost parts of Sweden began to emerge from the ice about 12,000 B.C. This is the oldest date in Swedish history and perhaps the oldest dependable one in the history of the world.

The primitive tribes who followed the ice as it withdrew northward carried on the first and decisive struggle for a settlement on Swedish soil. About 3,000 B.C. agriculture was begun. Imposing tombs made with huge blocks of stone enable us to trace the spread of this early peasant culture.

Copper and bronze became known about 1500 B. C., and the Bronze Age can be studied in the lavishly ornamented weapons and adornments which have been preserved in the soil. Common and extensive use of a metal in this early civilization was not possible until relations with countries to the south had acquainted the northerners with iron, which they learned to extract from

LEFT, *Sweden has many striking rock-carvings which were made in the solid rock about 2.500 to 3.000 years ago. The brave warriors in the picture are to be found on a rock in the province of Bohuslän. (Photo by* CLAES CLAESSON).

bog are found on the bottom of lakes and marshes. During the first centuries A.D. the provinces around Lake Mälaren and the *Suiones*, i.e., Svear, residing there began to assume their leading position. The first recorded mention of the *Suiones*, who were to give the whole country their name, is found in the *Germania* written by the Roman historian Tacitus in 98 A.D.

THE VIKING AGE AND EARLY CHRISTIANITY

The comparative isolation of Scandinavia was not broken until the Viking Age (700-1000 A. D.), when intrepid travellers brought back foreign goods and knowledge, new methods and new thoughts, in short, the contributions of more southerly civilizations. The coastal regions around and north of present-day Stockholm were the base of viking power and the starting point for great forays and trading expeditions—sometimes involving hundreds of ships—to the east. Whether as plunderers or merchants—and no clear distinction appears to have been made—the vikings kept up the contact between Sweden and the East (Russia, Constantinople), Sweden and Western Europe, including the British Isles and Ireland. The latter countries were the favourite goals of the men from southern Sweden who joined with Danish and Norwegian vikings, then their countrymen, in pillage, trade, or conquest.

Calmer centuries followed the viking expeditions and their tremendous display of energy. Eastern contacts ceased, and Sweden turned instead to the west and the south. Christianity gradually made headway with the aid of missions sent from England and northern Germany. Churches were built, first of wood, then of stone. Several hundreds of the latter from the twelfth and thirteenth centuries still stand. Sweden was incorporated in the huge organization of the Roman Catholic Church. At the same time the realm became more firmly established; it included Finland and all of modern Sweden, except the provinces of Blekinge, Bohuslän, Halland, and Skåne. Rival dynasties did not succeed in breaking the fundamental unity, definite procedures for electing the rulers were established, and a Council, drawn from the foremost families of the country, took its place by the king's side. Villages were expanded and new ones founded; in each century the frontier was pushed a little farther into the wilderness. During the thirteenth century the provincial statutes were compiled in law books which remain unique in their

LEFT, *Sweden has more than 2.000 rune stones, most of them inscribed in the eleventh century A. D. in memory of a dead person, sometimes a warrior who had fallen in a raid on England. The picture shows a rune stone at Lena Church in Uppland.*

age and clarity. By these the life of the whole province was regulated in detail from the most elevated aspects to the commonest everyday concerns: "Christ is foremost in our law, next to Him our Christian dogma and all Christians: the King, peasants and all legal residents, bishops, all men of booklearning", but also "if horse rolls or swine roots in grainfield, [owner] pays fine therefore with such grain as was sown in the field, one skep for every third rolling or every third rooting." Differentiation into social groups took place in this period; in addition to the clergy a class of nobles emerged, the latter composed of estate owners and those high in the service of kings or lords. The nobles were exempt from taxes in exchange for military service in heavy armour.

On the island of Gotland the town of Visby developed into one of the strongest members of the Hanseatic League. Sweden thereby gained full entry to European trading and obtained an international market for her products, such as copper, iron, butter, and pelts. Soon after 1350 a national code was compiled. Based in part on the provincial laws, it aimed above all to safeguard peace and personal security. Acts of violence in church, at the *ting*, personal attacks in another man's house or against a defenceless woman made a man an outlaw without rights and property. The "law of the land" included a brief constitution in which the powers of the king, the council, and the citizens were limited. Even in the modern world order the duties of the king could hardly be defined more succinctly than in the old text: "The King shall all justice and truth strengthen, love and preserve, all wrongs and falsehoods destroy, both by law and by his royal power."

Strangely, the first Swede of international stature was a woman. Saint Birgitta (or Bridget; 1303-1373) is the greatest medieval figure in both the religious and the literary history of Sweden. She founded a religious order which included both monks and nuns, and the first monastery was established at Vadstena. Visionary *(Revelationes)*, organizer (Order of St. Bridget), and unofficial envoy of Sweden in Rome for almost a quarter of a century, she also found time to be a devoted wife and busy mistress of the family estates for twenty-seven years. A child-bride at thirteen, she bore her husband eight children, one of whom became Saint Catherine of Sweden.

THE KALMAR UNION

Late in the fourteenth century Queen Margareta, daughter of one king and widow of another, ruled both Denmark and Norway. A general reaction against growing German influence in the country, the Swedish king then being the German, Albrekt of Mecklenburg, fear that their estates might be confiscated, and other circumstances prompted the Swedish nobles to appeal to Margareta for help against their own king. She defeated King Albrekt in

This and the following pages illustrate romantic reconstructions of important events in Swedish history and the kings who produced them. ABOVE, *Gustav Vasa at Mora incites the people to the insurrection which led to his enthronement and to the Reformation. From a painting by J. G. Sandberg (1782-1854) in the National Museum of Art, Stockholm.*

BELOW, *Gustav Vasa's triumphal entry into Stockholm after his peasant army had defeated the Danes. From a mural painting by Carl Larsson in the National Museum of Art, Stockholm (1853-1919).*

This huge battle scene by the well-known Swedish painter Carl Wahlbom (1810-1858) in the National

Museum, Stockholm, depicts the death of Gustav II Adolf in the thick of the fighting at Lützen in 1632.

ABOVE, *the corpse of Karl XII is borne home to Stockholm from Norway. From a painting by Gustaf Cederström (1845-1933), now in the Museum of Art, Gothenburg.*

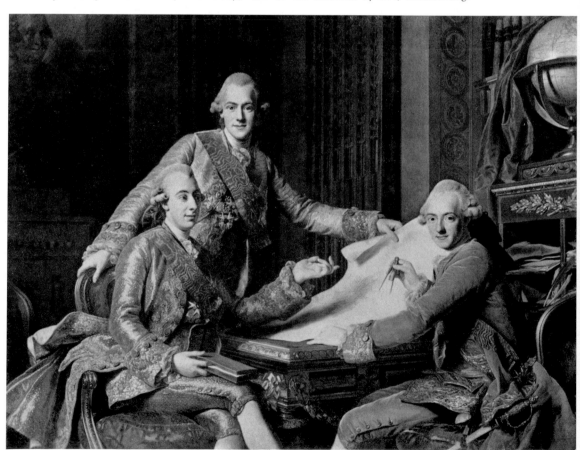

battle in 1389 and became mistress of a united Scandinavia. Negotiations conducted in the Swedish town of Kalmar in 1397 gave the Union its name.

Margareta's kingdom was Europe's largest in area. As a noble experiment the unified realm showed foresight and statesmanship, but after several decades of strife it failed nevertheless. Margareta's successor in 1412 (and nominal king since 1396), Erik of Pomerania, sought to extend the royal power throughout the triple realm and fought the German princes as well as the Hanseatic League while seeking political alliances in England and elsewhere. But Sweden was dependent on the Hanseatic League, especially in maintaining a market for her metals; furthermore, the country was little inclined to tolerate increased tyrannical power on the part of the king.

In the mining districts of Bergslagen the people rose in revolt under the leadership of a simple mine owner by the name of Engelbrekt. The nobles, viewing with alarm the king's bid for greater power, made common cause with him. After bitter struggles between Denmark and Sweden the Union was dissolved. During these turbulent decades in the fifteenth century a notable innovation was made in the Swedish political system: the *Riksdag*, or Parliament, was instituted, which on behalf of the people made important political decisions. Even the peasants were represented in this new body.

Christian II, king of Denmark since 1513, soom became a new threat to Sweden's independence. Hope of a successful defence against the repeated attacks faded when the Swedish regent, Sten Sture the Younger, fell in one of the losing battles against the Danes in 1520. By the "Stockholm Massacre", a mass execution in the conquered capital, Christian attempted to eliminate the leaders of the independence party and with them all opposition. Once more it appeared that a great northern kingdom was in formation, this time by violence. But the king had underestimated the Swedish tradition of freedom.

THE AGE OF GUSTAV VASA

A revolt against the Danish king, led by a young, rather unknown relative of the Stures, Gustav Eriksson Vasa, began in Dalarna in 1520-1521. Vasa definitely put an end to the Union and made Sweden into a national state of the type which had arisen on the Continent during the late Middle Ages. His features are familiar to every Swede and have become known to foreign visitors, for his portrait appears on Swedish paper money.

Gustav Vasa placed the stamp of his personality on Sweden's history from

LEFT, *Gustav III and his brothers confer over a military map. The man with the book is the king. From a painting by Alexander Roslin (1718-1793), now in the National Museum, Stockholm.*

1523, when at the age of twenty-seven he was elected to the throne, until his death in 1560. His first royal concern was the stabilization of the state finances; by resolute measures at the Västerås *Riksdag* in 1527 he created the conditions necessary for the confiscation by the state of all property in the hands of the Roman Catholic Church. Since at the end of the Middle Ages the Church held 21 % of the Swedish soil, as compared with only 5.6 % owned by the Crown, this represented an immense addition to the strength of the state. Gustav Vasa found a certain amount of justification for this measure in the Lutheran teachings which had begun to spread in the country with the full approval of the king. Gradually the Swedish Church was separated from Rome, became Lutheran in character, and was organized into a state Church which survives to this day. The decree of the Västerås Parliament established the new religious phase with the goodly statement that "the plain and true word of God shall be preached in the realm." Simultaneously with the great confiscation of church property the king and his men reorganized the government administration and developed unprecedented efficiency. Various provinces, such as Dalarna and Småland, objected strenuously to having their local interests set aside for the common good. When they rebelled against the king, they were severely castigated. Foundations for modern literature were also laid during the reign of Gustav Vasa with a complete translation of the Bible and in the hymns and theological writings of Olaus Petri, Swedish reformer.

For half a century his sons, Erik XIV, Johan III, and Karl IX, ruled Sweden in the order named. All three were interesting, talented, but contradictory men, engrossed in the confusing international relations of the day. From the south, Denmark plotted against Sweden, while the Swedes repeatedly waged war against Lübeck, Poland, and Russia. One of their more consistent efforts was to gain control over Russia's foreign trade in the Baltic Sea, to which she had no direct access. When Estonia became Swedish in 1595, this objective was partly attained, for Sweden thereby obtained considerable strength in the Baltic area and control over some of the important trade routes to Russia.

A new attempt at a north-European union was made by Sigismund, son of Johan III, who through his mother first became king of Poland, then in 1592 succeeded his father on the throne of Sweden. His Catholicism and prolonged absences in Poland caused great opposition in Sweden and paved the way for his uncle Karl to depose him in 1599. The only consequence of Sigismund's abortive enterprise was that acute enmity replaced the former alliance between the two countries. Karl remained protector of the realm and did not assume the title of King Karl IX until 1604. During the last years before his death in 1611 Sweden was waging a losing struggle against Denmark, Poland, and Russia. The situation looked dark indeed.

One of the reasons why Sweden became a great power in Europe was that the Swedes learned how to make use of the great iron-ore deposits of the country. The picture shows iron-mines at Nordmark, Värmland. Water-colour by Fredrik Adolf von Numers (1745-1792).

GUSTAV II ADOLF

Sweden's greatest expansion grew out of the ensuing struggle for existence. Even Karl IX's campaigns against Sigismund and Poland had acquired an expansionist character, but the new conflict spread to include all of Europe in the Thirty Years' War. The House of Habsburg was in the process of crushing the Protestant princes in Germany and advanced toward the Baltic with the aim of becoming a great power also in northern Europe. Gustav Adolf decided to participate in the historic struggle. He first launched an attack against Poland and seized the most important towns in eastern Prussia, which were vital to Poland's commerce. Then he led his army into Germany against Habsburg and the Catholic League, received support from France, and in 1631 routed the famous General Tilly in the battle of Breitenfeld (near Leipzig) in Saxony. The next winter he held court in Mainz and Frankfurt a.M., marched through Bavaria in the summer of 1632, and on the 6th of November that year encountered Wallenstein, the Emperors' chief commander, at Lützen, not far from Breitenfeld. Wallenstein was forced to retreat, but Gustav Adolf fell in the battle.

An almost inevitable question presents itself as these extensive campaigns are reviewed: How could a small country like Sweden, modest in its resources, generate and maintain such military power?

Throughout the war the king had the people's approval. Parliament, including nobles, clergy, burghers, and peasants, had been in full accord with him on the necessity of entering the war in Germany. In presenting and justifying his plans and actions before the representatives of the people the king was indefatigable. His armies were largely composed of Swedish farmers, their sons and hands. A source of financial support was the copper mine at Falun, whose exports were then in great demand throughout Europe. The political genius of Gustav II Adolf, his talent for military organization, and his advanced ideas on strategy and tactics were important contributory factors in the success of his campaigns. In addition, the king possessed outstanding administrative ability.

When Gustav Adolf fell, his heir and only child, Kristina, was six years old. The regency was placed in the hands of a group from the upper nobility, headed by Chancellor Axel Oxenstierna, Sweden's greatest statesman. For sixteen more years the war in Germany continued. The Peace of Westphalia (1648) gave to Sweden a number of important possessions on the southern shore of the Baltic and on the North Sea, but the Polish ports had to be

RIGHT, *King Karl XIV Johan, during whose reign the old project for a canal through Sweden was realized. Engraving by P. M. Alix (1752-1819).*

relinquished; in addition, the Catholic German states were to pay reparations.

Sweden's strategic position was entirely changed. Queen Kristina abdicated in 1654 and was succeeded by her cousin, Karl X Gustav, who was waging war in Poland when Denmark joined Sweden's enemies. He then departed from Poland with his army in 1658, marched through Schleswig-Holstein and forced the Danes to transfer to Sweden the provinces of Blekinge, Skåne, Halland, and Bohuslän. In a surprise move the king had led his army over the newly frozen Belts—one of history's most daring exploits—and Denmark had to relinquish her control over the Sound, main inlet to the Baltic Sea.

SOCIAL CRISIS — KARL XI's FINANCIAL REORGANIZATION

Since that time the southern provinces have remained Swedish and represent the lasting gain from the period of power politics. However, this policy also had a very negative aspect. A large portion of the monies and much of the support needed for the wars had been secured through the transfer or sale of crown lands or tax concessions to the nobility. In a country still having an economy largely operating in kind, resort to such means was necessary. European power politics could not, after all, be financed with taxes paid in butter and grain. The result was that the nobles ended up with the possession of about 72 % of Sweden's soil, while the Crown and the independent farmers had to be satisfied with the remaining 28 %. Those farmers who had become subject to the nobles and paid their taxes to them obviously had difficulty in maintaining any measure of independence, especially since the lords in question had acquired on the Continent a purely feudal attitude toward subordinates. Enormous as the growth was in the wealth and political influence of the nobles, it had its justification in the brilliant contributions made by them during the war period. Nevertheless, it became a source of danger to the existence of free husbandmen as well as to the central government authorities.

Sweden's Vasa kings had not always seen eye to eye with the nobles. Gustav Vasa's three sons had severe clashes and sanguinary reckonings with them. Gustav II Adolf had maintained good cooperation with the great men of the realm, but for his daughter, Kristina, the situation was more difficult. To curb the nobles, restore order in the state finances after the wars, and assist the peasants in the struggle for their ancient freedoms combined into an immense task even for so talented a woman ruler as Kristina. Furthermore, her personal position was changed when she secretly became a convert to Catholicism. She found herself in a complex quandary of conscience and decided to abdicate, but not until she had secured the throne for her

38

cousin, Karl Gustav, and forestalled his being faced with increased power on the part of the nobility. The almost constant wars and his early death (1660) at the age of thirty-eight prevented Karl X Gustav, too, from solving the great internal problems. During the long regency for his minor son, Karl XI, the influence of the nobles grew even more. Early in Karl XI's own reign, which began in 1672, he had to lead a bitter struggle against Denmark for the retention of the southern provinces. When peace was concluded in 1679, the king began a gigantic task of reorganization reminiscent of Gustav Vasa's a century and a half earlier. This is customarily referred to as Karl XI's "reduction," i.e., by vote of Parliament the nobles were "reduced" as the Crown repossessed a large part of the estates they had obtained for themselves. At the end of this reorganization the property distribution was once more radically changed; the Crown now held 35.6 % of the soil, the nobles only 32.9 %, and the independent farmers 31,5 %. In accordance with a detailed plan, the king used the income from state properties to cover all expenses of the Crown, such as the military and civil service payrolls. An important byproduct of the reorganization was that the status of the freeholders was restored and secured. The nobles retained their extensive privileges, but their rule was replaced by that of an absolute monarch.

A few years of peace quickened the economic life of the nation. Copper had declined in importance, but iron exports had increased, and wood tar also became a major item in the shipments abroad at the time. This peaceful period gave Karl XI an opportunity to carry out his sometimes harsh but generally beneficial reforms. They affected every phase of Swedish life: commerce, finance, defence, legal procedure, the Church, and education.

KARL XII

Nearly two decades of peace under Karl XI were followed by the last major war period in Sweden's history. Upon the death of his father in 1697, Karl XII, just past fifteen, at the urging of Parliament ascended the throne as ruling and absolute monarch.

Two years later the storm broke as Sweden was threatened by a triple attack; Russia, Poland-Saxony, and Denmark declared war, and Sweden's situation seemed as difficult as it had been a hundred years earlier. In brilliant victories—the most famous in 1700 at Narva aginst Russian forces ten times as great—Karl frustrated the plans of the hostile coalition, eliminated Denmark, gave the Czar the setback at Narva, pursued the Polish King August through Poland, and forced the Peace of Altranstädt in 1706.

A bold expedition against Russia's heart in 1709 anticipated the trail of both Napoleon and Hitler; in each case the outcome was about the same. It led to Karl's defeat at Poltava, the capitulation of his army, and his own flight to Turkey. There he was virtually interned for years, during which he was partly successful in persuading the Turks to attack Russia. The home country held out against the extended coalition which now included Russia, Saxony, Denmark, Hanover, England, and Prussia. In 1715 the king managed to return to Sweden.

Karl pinned his hopes on the Anglo-Russian rivalry, but in the midst of complicated diplomatic manœuvres he was killed as he besieged the Norwegian fortress of Fredriksten (near Fredrikshald) in 1718. Sweden then had to conclude a series of peace treaties which left her with few of her far-flung possessions, except most of Finland and a couple of small holdings on the south shore of the Baltic. Again Sweden's situation was completely changed.

"ERA OF LIBERTY"—INTRODUCTION OF PARLIAMENTARIANISM

A total but almost bloodless revolution to establish a new constitution was the first internal move after the collapse. This gave by far the greatest authority to Parliament, whose wishes were carried out by the king and his council. In the council the king had only two votes, and he was himself elected to the throne by Parliament.

The "Era of Liberty," as the next fifty-three years are called, has been severely criticized for its partisan animosity and political befuddlement. But it has become increasingly clear that this era was of great significance in shaping the Swedish heritage of freedom. A real parliamentary system was gradually developed, which to be sure laboured under very heavy and cumbersome procedures. Nevertheless, it is of great interest in many respects and a notable parallel to the English system.

Two parties, the Hats and the Caps, came into being and contended for the political power. In their theories of national economy the Hats were strictly mercantilistic. Their foreign policy aimed at an alliance with France whereby they hoped to regain the foreign possessions recently lost; this led to badly prepared wars with unfortunate outcomes.

The Caps were more restrained about state subsidies in the national economy, and their foreign policy strove for rapprochement with England and Russia. Towards the end of the era the Caps gathered into their ranks the commoners in opposition to the nobles.

RIGHT, *in the first half of the nineteenth century country people in Sweden wore gaily-coloured costumes like this. Even to-day such peasant costumes are used for local festivities. The picture shows country people outside Lund Cathedral. Oil-painting by O. H. Wallgren (1795-1857), in Östergötland Museum.*

Alternately in power—the Hats being at the helm somewhat longer—the two parties developed far-reaching assumptions regarding the authority of Parliament. "The idea that the Estates (of Parliament) may err is contrary to the fundamental law of the realm" is a sample of their claims; if the king refused to sign the council decisions, a facsimile stamp of the royal signature was sometimes used. During these years of acrid party feuds, however, a truly significant political development took place which proved of great importance to the subsequent evolution of the Swedish constitution. Considerable economic and cultural progress also characterized the era. A canal from Lake Vänern to Kattegatt, planned during the last years of Karl XII, was begun. Land reforms came under discussion, there was an interest in the advancement of science, and the Swedish press was born. Carl von Linné (Linnaeus) created his botanical classification system, and Emanuel Swedenborg his unique philosophy of religion.

Violent struggles over the prerogatives of the nobility flared up during the last years of the Era of Liberty. The foreign policy of the Hats had cost Sweden a part of Finland. A certain weariness with the constant tug-of-war between the two parties was in evidence. All in all, a number of circumstances paved the way for a new *coup d'état*.

THE GUSTAVIAN PERIOD

Gustav III, a nephew of Prussia's Frederick the Great, ascended the throne in 1771. The following year he placed himself at the head of the forces opposed to the *status quo*, and the ensuing revolution took place without bloodshed. A new constitution accorded the king greater power, but he could not overrule all parliamentary opposition, least of all that of the politically powerful nobility. Consequently, in the midst of a provoked and ill conducted war with Russia, Gustav III achieved a second *coup* which increased the royal prerogatives to such an extent that the next twenty years (1789-1809) are referred to as the "Gustavian Absolutism". Gustav III himself was assassinated three years later (1792) by a fanatical group of young noblemen in the opposition. A patron of literature and the arts, endowed with brilliant personal qualities, Gustav III remains one of the most captivating and colourful figures in the whole succession of Swedish rulers.

This period brought certain important reforms, among them an equalization of civil rights and a fundamental land act, but the external events became predominant. In 1805 Gustav IV Adolf, son and heir of Gustav III, had chosen to side with England in the contest for supremacy among the great powers. Thus Sweden was drawn into the struggle against Napoleon and soon found herself in an extremely precarious situation. The king took this step with an eye to England's great importance in Sweden's foreign trade and stood firm in spite of Napoleon's overwhelming success. The outcome was nearly catastrophic.

In the Treaty of Tilsit (1807), Napoleon gave his new ally, Alexander I of Russia, a free hand to proceed against Sweden, hoping to force her into the camp of England's enemies. The aim was to make the Continental Blockade against England wholly effective. As Gustav IV Adolf remained loyal to his ally, Russia fell upon Finland, which was lost in its entirety (1809). Gustav IV Adolf's ability was by no means great enough to meet the crisis, and his temperament further emphasized the absolute nature of his office. In the eyes of the public officials, the military, and all liberty-professing citizens he became the scapegoat for the unhappy outcome and was removed in a new revolution, (1809), again without bloodshed. A new constitution was adopted, which in its fundamental features is still in effect, and the deposed king's uncle became ruler as Karl XIII. During these years of crisis and defeat first plans for a waterway from Lake Vänern to the Baltic Sea were laid; the work was completed twenty years later (1832).

CONSTITUTIONAL DEVELOPMENT

Since 1521 Sweden had undergone six major dynastic or constitutional readjustments, the last four without bloodshed. Within the same three hundred years she went through three sweeping changes of a social nature, for the most part peacefully. Gustav Vasa's confiscation of church property and Karl XI's repossession of crown lands have already been traced; the third social change spanned the years 1719-1809 and may be described as a gradual and more equitable redistribution of rights and privileges.

What the French Revolution achieved by means of numerous violent upheavals came about undramatically but quite effectively in Sweden. For example, the farmers obtained the right to purchase clear title to crown lands. Commoners could own exempt land and were admitted even to high government posts previously held only by nobles. Several of these innovations were made by Gustav III. Some archaic elements remained in the constitution and the social structure, however, and the political struggles of the nineteenth century pivoted to a large extent around them.

In the Constitution of 1809 the attempt was made to profit from previous experience in achieving a balance among the various authorities: king, cabinet, parliament, and government officials. The success of this attempt depended in part on the leaders involved.

Karl XIII was childless, and a successor had to be found outside the dynasty. The final choice was one of Napoleon's famous marshals, Bernadotte, who became Crown Prince Karl Johan when he set foot on Swedish soil in 1810. By involving his adopted country in the last coalition against

Napoleon, he obtained compensation of a sort for the loss of Finland. In exchange for Swedish Pomerania, the last of Sweden's possessions in northern Germany, Denmark was forced to relinquish Norway to Sweden. The Norwegians protested, chose their own king, and drew up a new constitution for themselves. They were finally compelled to accept a union with Sweden in 1814, but their virtual independence and the recently adopted constitution were both recognized. This chain of events gained considerable authority for Karl Johan, and his personal influence buttressed the royal power. On the death of the old king in 1818, the French marshal and former sergeant became Karl XIV Johan.

There was growing class consciousness on the part of the middle class which had emerged during the past hundred years. It included modern entrepreneurs in commerce, agriculture, and such industry as existed. Within the framework of the constitution a struggle now ensued concerning public influence on the country's administration, and liberal opinion really came to the fore in the 1840's. In the reigns of Oscar I and Karl XV—son and grandson, respectively, of Karl XIV Johan—a series of reforms were carried out. Most important among these was the change in national representation of 1865. It abolished the four Estates—nobles, clergy, burghers, and peasants—of which the Swedish Parliament had traditionally been composed, as no longer representative of the existing social structure. Instead the *Riksdag* was to have two elected chambers. Free enterprise became a normal part of the Swedish system in 1846, free trade in the 1860's. Public schools and free education became general in 1842, and the manufacture of alcoholic liquors was restricted in 1854.

EMIGRATION AND INDUSTRIALIZATION

The greatest changes in nineteenth century Sweden are of such a nature that they cannot be traced in terms of specific dates. Since the middle of the eighteenth century the population had increased rapidly—it had approximately doubled by 1850—and the country's resources could not keep the pace. To be sure, it had been possible to modernize agriculture by means of the already-mentioned land reforms of the early nineteenth century. The ancient village units, whose collective work methods did not meet modern demands, were divided by the Enclosure Act into "individually operating farms." Much new land was cultivated and working methods were rationalized. But these gains in land and efficiency still could not keep pace with a constantly growing population. A rural proletariat came into being, which was faced with almost insoluble problems.

This brought about a great emigration, which began in the middle of the nineteenth century and culminated in the 1880's. The goal for most of those who left was the United States, where more space and greater opportunities beckoned. In the 1880's, a decade of agricultural depression, an alarming total of 347,000 Swedes emigrated; 46,900 departed in the peak year (1887). In America the immigrants frequently settled all-Swedish communities, some of which still exist as such. They often sought out territory which in climate, terrain, and resources resembled the home province and thus offered similar opportunities for earning a livelihood; the preponderantly Swedish communities in north central United States are in many ways reminiscent of Sweden. The greatest concentration of Swedish immigrants settled in the area west of Lake Michigan as far out as the Rocky Mountains, from the southern edge of Kansas up to the Canadian border. Naturally, Swedes in smaller numbers are found in all parts of the United States.

Their early predecessors were the Swedes who in 1638 established a Swedish colony, New Sweden, near the present city of Wilmington on the Delaware. A descendant of these first Swedish-Americans was John Morton, one of those who signed the Declaration of Independence.

Gradually the tide of emigration receded, largely as a result of another major change in the social structure. The beginnings of modern industry had been in evidence as early as the middle of the nineteenth century. In the lead were the forest industries; demand for lumber from the great Swedish stands was soon found abroad, as modern, steam-powered sawmills were erected. Industrialization proceeded at a more rapid rate from about 1870 and definitely reached the front rank in the national economy around 1890. Parts of ancient, agricultural Sweden now became big modern industrial regions. Formerly the frontier could be moved only by breaking new land or working new mines. Now, however, men could penetrate into the remotest wilderness and exploit its long-hidden resources. Added to this were the metal industries previously described and other manufacturing activities. New technological processes were at last developed which towards the end of the nineteenth century made the formerly worthless, high-phosphorus ore of northern Sweden with its rich iron content a very important export staple.

Parallel with this economic revolution—the greatest in Sweden's history since the establishment of agriculture in the Stone Age—a new and extensive social change was taking place; the term "popular movements" is commonly used to describe it. The great groups of the population who did not have the suffrage—and only 9.5 % were entitled to vote even at the beginning of the twentieth century—began to seek other outlets for their energy and new ways to exert an influence on the society in which they lived. They found such outlets in the religious revival movements in the middle of the century; in the labour movement, which grew rapidly during the decades of industrialization and early embraced social democracy as its political faith; in the temperance movements, which became a great force in the social training and education of the so-called lower classes; and later they turned to the cooperative movement and organized sports.

UNIVERSAL SUFFRAGE

These social trends and the general concern of the people with problems of national interest led to a whole series of constitutional changes and social reforms. When the union with Norway was dissolved in 1905—another major adjustment made in a peaceable and dignified manner—solution of the internal problems became even more urgent. A franchise reform in 1907 doubled the electorate from 9.5 % to 19 % of the total population. Complete democracy with universal suffrage for men and women, making over 54 % of the citizens voters, was achieved in 1918. Political parties in the modern sense began to emerge late in the last century; they were strong and active in the early decades of the present one. Parliamentarianism first came to the fore in modern times in 1905 and became definitively established in 1917. Social welfare legislation began in earnest early in the present century and started to make rapid strides along partly new lines of approach in the 1930's. The results were achieved on the basis of a general debate in which all the parties of the *Riksdag*—Conservatives, Liberals, and Social Democrats—participated.

Most heatedly discussed were the problems of labour and unemployment. The creation of a modern military establishment was begun towards the end of the nineteenth century but later became the subject of very conflicting opinions. Real unity of purpose was not attained until the 1930's and then under the pressure of the dictatorship to the south.

The great social and economic changes which have taken place since the middle of the last century have been achieved along constitutional and legislative lines without violent upheavals. Sometimes they have been slow and deliberate but by way of compensation well considered and in harmony with the legal heritage of Sweden.

WORLD WAR II

When the war began, Sweden, in concurrence with the other northern countries, issued a declaration of neutrality which almost immediately had to meet its first test during the Finno-Russian war in the winter of 1939-1940. A strong popular movement in favour of Finland's cause then made itself felt but did not result in any official participation in the conflict. On the other hand, a number of volunteers joined the Finnish forces, and Sweden placed extensive material aid at Finland's disposal. When later the Allies, primarily England, wished to send troops through Sweden to aid Finland (March, 1940), the request was refused. This was motivated by the government's desire to prevent the country's being drawn into the conflict between the great powers. Towards the end of the "winter war" Sweden undertook the role of mediator between the two belligerents.

Close on the heels of the Finno-Russian armistice came the German occupation of Denmark and the attack on Norway (April 9, 1940). German plans to attack Sweden as well were known to exist; Sweden's rearmament was not completed and her strategic situation extremely difficult. How to resist the German demands for permission to send military transports over Swedish territory against the defenders of Norway became a serious problem. Such demands were repeatedly turned down in April and May, 1940, and only Red Cross transports to northern Norway were permitted. After Germany had occupied Norway, the government felt constrained to permit transit of military equipment and personnel on leave between Norway and Germany via Sweden. Both the government and the high command were convinced at that time that a hopeless war with Germany would have been unavoidable if the demands had been refused. In many quarters the reaction of public opinion was very strong. A popular movement on behalf of Norway's cause gathered numerous supporters in the months that followed, and the Swedish people became aware of a deep strain on their conscience in this tragic situation.

The government was forced to make one more major concession to the Nazis. Just before the German attack on Russia in June, 1941, the transfer of a German division from Norway to Finland over Swedish territory was permitted. Further requests of that nature were refused.

The Swedish people had to realize that they were living in threatened, but still independent, isolation in the north European sphere of German conquest. Only with great difficulty was it possible to tide the nation over the shortages, as extensive rationing and a speedy conversion of industry were effected. Ships given safe conduct by both belligerent sides maintained some contact with the outside world, and a certain amount of trade was carried on with Germany. On April 9, 1940, about one half of the Swedish merchant marine was in foreign waters outside the German blockade; this tonnage was chartered to England and the United States.

The Swedish iron ore export to Germany had to be carried on. It was of utmost importance for Sweden to be able to import coal, coke, and fertilizers. A drastic reduction of the iron ore export to Germany might also have led to increased pressure by the Nazis.

When after 1942 the general picture slowly changed, Sweden's delicate position was improved. Sweden had also been able to build up her defences. This increased the freedom of action and made it possible in August, 1943, to bring the transit of military material and personnel between Norway and Germany to an end. The Germans protested in vain. A new trade agreement with the Allies was concluded, and the iron ore export to Germany was cut from 10 to 7.5 million tons.

During the final stages of the European war Sweden became increasingly active in humanitarian work. Much had, of course, been done ever since the outbreak of hostilities; thus in 1939-1940 during the "winter war" many Finnish children were received and cared for in Swedish homes. When the Germans attacked Norway, a stream of refugees began to flow into Sweden and finally totalled about 50,000. Some of these went on to Allied countries; around 5,800 went by air to England. Some of the Norwegians and Danes were also trained in Sweden for later military police duty, fully equipped and armed.

Large numbers of refugees from the Baltic countries to the east were also admitted during the war years. When the Nazi pogroms against Danish Jews began, approximately 7,500 found asylum in Sweden. King Gustav V addressed a profound personal plea to the Nazi government in Budapest, asking for humane treatment of the Hungarian Jews. The Swedish Legation in Budapest attracted international attention as emergency passports were issued to thousands of persecuted Jews. After long and intricate negotiations with the Germans further aid became possible in an unexpected manner. Count Folke Bernadotte (1895-1948), a nephew of the king, organized in the spring of 1945 the removal of the Danes and Norwegians—and later prisoners of other nationalities—from the German concentration camps and their transportation to Sweden. With a caravan of buses the Swedish Red Cross carried out the adventurous plan.

THE 1950—1960 DECADE

Sweden's position between the spheres of interest dominated by the two major power blocs has prompted the political leadership to adhere to the course of neutrality, which has been of obvious advantage in the past. This seemed especially pertinent when the question of joining the North Atlantic Treaty Organization (NATO) was discussed, as well as when the attempts to form a northern defense alliance failed. By and large, the Swed-

TOP RIGHT, *the Swedish King and his family play an important role in Swedish official life. Here he hands over a Nobel Prize in the Stockholm Concert Hall. The royal party in the front row: Prince Bertil, Queen Louise, Princess Sibylla and her daughters Margaretha and Christina.*—BELOW: *the solemn opening of the Riksdag with the King surrounded by members of the Government, high civil servants and officers.*

ish people are united on the principle of neutrality, but the relations with the other northern countries have not been in any way impaired by this stand. To aid cooperation among the nations of the North, the Nordic Council, established in 1953, offers a forum for discussions by representatives of the respective governments and parliaments.

The social reforms have been advanced in accordance with previously formulated plans, and the political parties are in agreement on the essential aspects involved. The most notable steps taken in recent years have been the reorganization of the school system, establishing *enhetsskolan*, a "comprehensive" elementary schooling of nine years; increases in old-age pensions; the change of the ancient rural parishes into larger, combined units, *storkommuner*, which more adequately meet modern administrative requirements; and the abolition of the passbook for the purchase of alcoholic beverages, prompted by a more liberal interpretation of the alcohol problem on the part of the government authorities. In 1959, after lengthy discussions, a decision was made in favour of general, so-called service pensions. It should also be mentioned that Sweden's defences have been modernized and enlarged with the acquiescence of all political parties but not without heated debates on technical and strategic problems.

Sweden's economy has to a certain extent reflected the international state of affairs. Among the characteristic features are a continued period of prosperity, a government policy deliberately aimed to achieve full employment, a general and manifest rise in the standard of living, and a somewhat spasmodic inflation. The country's financial policies have especially been the subject of lively debates, and many means have been tried to bring the inflationary tendencies under control or, hopefully, eliminate them altogether. In 1959 Sweden took an active part in the creation of the European Free Trade Association (EFTA). Since Sweden's economy is dependent on all-European trade, means are being sought to establish working relations with the European Common Market, which absorbs 32 % of Sweden's trade.

Tage Erlander has been prime minister since 1946. The Social Democratic government was reorganized early in 1951 into a coalition with the Center Party. In 1957 this coalition was replaced with a new, wholly Social Democratic cabinet.

Sweden's monarch, Gustaf V, died in 1950 at the age of ninety-two, after a reign of forty-three years. He was succeeded on the throne by his oldest son, Gustaf VI Adolf, whose royal motto is "Duty Above All."

THE GÖTA CANAL

AND HOW IT WAS BUILT

Desiné et gravé par A. F. S.

ABOVE, *a 1804 print by A. F. Skjöldebrand which dramatises the great cataract at Trollhättan.*—ON PREVIOUS PAGE, *since early times travellers have remarked on the great waterfall at Trollhättan. The picture is an engraving, published in a book of 1658 by the learned Dutchman, Johannes Herbinius.*

THE GÖTA CANAL AND HOW IT WAS BUILT

The name Göta Canal is often given to the entire navigation between
Gothenburg and Stockholm, but this is a misnomer. The entire navigation
is composed of a number of waterways. Starting from Gothenburg we
proceed for about 55 miles up the wide, canalised Göta Älv (River); at
Trollhättan we ascend the great staircase of locks, thence through the old
Karls Grav canal and into Lake Vänern. That is the first stage of the
journey and is often called as a whole the Trollhätte Canal, though it is
composed mainly of the Göta River. At Sjötorp, on the eastern shore of
Lake Vänern, the Göta Canal proper begins and runs eastwards for 114
miles to Mem on the Baltic Sea   first as the Western Line through Västergötland into Lake Vättern and then as the Eastern Line through Östergötland. From Slätbaken, an arm of the Baltic, vessels pass through the Östergötland and the Södermanland archipelago, then turn northwards into a
fjord, pass through the two-mile-long Södertälje Canal into Lake Mälaren,
thence eastward to Stockholm.

The whole journey, which can be made by steamer in either direction, is
347 miles long. Most of the length consists of lakes and rivers, but about
60 miles are composed of man-made cuts through soil and rock, and about
50 miles is in the open Baltic Sea. Along the route 65 locks raise vessels
304 feet above sea level over Sweden's central ridge and lower them down
to sea level again. The Trollhätte Canal, which is older than the Göta Canal,
now has the most modern and the biggest locks—big enough to take sea-
going ships and all operated by power from the Trollhätte hydro-electric
works. The Göta Canal proper between Sjötorp and Mem has smaller locks
which are still worked by hand just as they were when the canal was completed in 1832. On this navigation the old intimate charm of the early
nineteenth-century waterways persists and this is perhaps the most beautiful
and enjoyable part of the journey.

If you are restless and hurried you must travel between Gothenburg and
Stockholm by train or plane, but if you want to gain an impression of
Swedish landscape, history, and culture as revealed in a typical cross-

section of the country in a smooth and restful way, then make this summer trip by passenger steamer on the Göta Canal route which takes two-and-a-half days. The small, white steamers are comfortable, the food aboard is excellent and you will have frequent opportunities to step ashore to stretch your legs and to explore. The scenery is beautiful and varies between open lake or sea and intimate, leafy cut.

HISTORY OF THE WATERWAY

The uniting of the North Sea with the Baltic by a waterway right across the country had been a Swedish dream ever since Bishop Hans Brask of Linköping put forward a project early in the sixteenth century. When Brask fled the country at the Reformation, King Gustavus Vasa made an abortive attempt to carry out part of the bishop's scheme by joining Lake Roxen with the Baltic via Söderköping, which was then an important port. His son John (Johan) began the digging of this canal, and its remains, called Braskens Grav, can still be seen just to the north of the present canal at Norsholm.

In 1607 a lock at Lilla Edet on the Göta River was built and about this time too the Karls Grav between Lake Vänern and the Göta River was dug to enable ships to pass the Rånnum waterfalls, the first on the Göta River below Lake Vänern. That was in the reign of Charles IX. Karls Grav, though modernised, remains Sweden's oldest navigable canal.

When Sweden gained some control of the sound between Sweden and Denmark with the Peace of Roskilde in 1658, the need for a cross-country canal, which would free shipping from the tolls and the dangers of the Sound, became less urgent and interest in the idea waned. In 1718, however, plans were again revived when Charles XII gave a contract to Christopher Polhem, Sweden's first engineer, to link the two seas by a waterway which would provide military as well as trading advantages. The contract stipulated, somewhat fantastically, that the navigation between Lake Vänern and the Göta River, past the great falls at Trollhättan, would be completed during the first three years, that in the fourth year Vättern and Vänern would be linked and in the fifth year Lake Vättern and the Baltic Sea—and all this with locks which were to be larger than those now existing on the Göta Canal. Work began at once under the direction of Polhem and Swedenborg, the famous scientist and mystic, but all work stopped when the king was killed in battle. Two locks hewn from the solid granite were actually constructed later at Trollhättan; one of them is now under water but the other

RIGHT, *a statue of the early engineer, Christopher Polhem, by Ivar Johnsson, erected in Gothenburg in 1952 (photo by* ERIC DE MARÉ).

54

Thomas Telford, F.R.S.

Engraved by W. Holl after the portrait, by Samuel Lane.

Published by John Murray Albemarle Street 1861.

An engraving of Thomas Telford, the Scottish engineer who was consulted on the construction of the Göta Canal.

A lithograph of Count Baltzar von Platen, the progenitor of the Göta Canal.

Some drawings from the archives of the Göta Canal Company at Motala, used in the early days of the canal. ABOVE, *the engine of a dredger, imported from England in 1822. The drawing is made by Nils Ericson.*

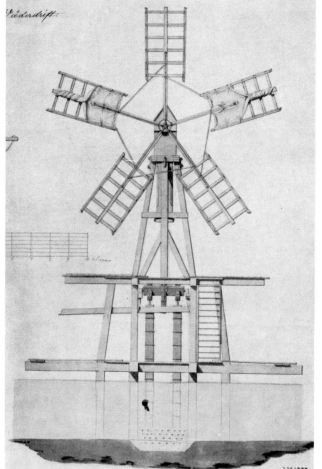

LEFT, *a wind pump.*

BELOW, *a revolving crane.*

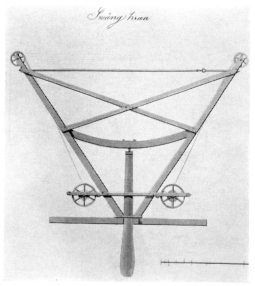

can still be seen and is called Polhem's Sluss (Lock). The Polhem scheme came to nothing in the end for, as the locks past the Trollhätte falls were nearing completion—the most hazardous and difficult part of the whole project—the dam burst and the work was ruined. A local legend relates that this was a deliberate piece of sabotage by the local peasants who were augmenting their meagre incomes from the soil by hauling cargoes round the falls by land.

Not until the year 1800 did great Vänern, the third largest lake in Europe, at last acquire a navigable outlet to the North Sea. Thirty-two years had still to pass, however, before the cross-country navigation was fully realised.

On the board of directors of the concern which had constructed the Troll-hätte Canal was a man named Platen—Admiral Count Baltzar Bogislaus von Platen (1766-1829). Encouraged by the success of the Trollhätte Canal, he began to think seriously about the old Swedish dream of a waterway right across the country, and in 1806, after some research, he published a work on canals in which he advocated the immediate construction of the complete cross-country navigation.

What sort of man was the Count? Though he was a competent naval officer in his younger days, when he was captured and interned in Russia for two years, and though he was to become a leading member of the Riksdag, his national fame rests mainly on his realisation of the Göta Canal. He was born an aristocrat on the island of Rügen in Pomerania, then a Swedish province, and he became a fervent Swedish patriot, not least in doggedly propounding his scheme of defensive strategy in which the building of the canal formed an essential element.

The building of the canal was the Count's life work. It might never have been accomplished if he had not inherited from his long line of Teuton ancestors a genius for organisation, a passionate, romantic but thoroughly practical nature, a patrician's initiative and a determination so firm that a modern psychiatrist would probably call it, with a moral shake of the head, "obsessional." One of his peers declared him to be "a liberal despot and a despotic liberal," perhaps because, although his views were far-sighted, progressive and disinterested, opposition to any line of action he had decided was right and proper was liable to produce in him an explosion of irascible but effective rhetoric. At the same time he seems to have been an amiable character of spontaneity, simplicity and integrity. His energy was tremendous.

Yet the Göta Canal needed more than the drive of a Platen to become a reality. It needed the skill and experience of a group of British craftsmen and overseers to control and instruct the regiments of Swedish infantrymen who were employed on the canal in their thousands during the years between 1810 and 1832 when the canal was building. It also needed the knowledge and advice of the foremost engineer in the world at that time—Thomas Telford (1757-1834), the Scot who was born in a remote croft in Dumfriesshire, was trained as a mason, lived to bring tremendous improvements to Britain's communications and died to be buried with honour in Westminster Abbey.

The basis of Platen's scheme was the line proposed and surveyed by Daniel af Thunberg and Elias Schweder in the 1780:ies, the principles being those of the English canal builders, notably Brindley, who believed, first, that rivers did not make good navigations in themselves but existed to supply canals with water and, secondly, that locks should be grouped together in the canals as far as possible. As Platen saw it, the canal, apart from its military importance and the independence it would give from the imposition of the tolls charged at the Sound between Sweden and Denmark, would be valuable for the transport of such materials as timber, grain, limestone, copper, herrings and salt and would greatly increase foreign trade, especially with England. Moreover it would form a main artery or Leader to which other navigations and canals in central Sweden could be directed. When Telford's Caledonian Canal had been completed a direct route for vessels would be available between the west coast of the British Isles and all the Baltic countries, including Russia. The Göta Canal, Platen considered, would be able to obtain at least five per cent of the merchant shipping which went through the Sound and that would provide ample profit.

In spite of Platen's acquired knowledge about canal construction and because of the great size of the project, it was decided that advice should be obtained from a British expert, Great Britain being at that time the country renowned for its new canals. On August 8th, 1808 Telford arrived in Sweden with two assistants and within the remarkably short time of 20 days the line was marked out and lock positions were fixed, with, as a contemporary remarked, "absolutely incomparable, diligence, perseverance and drive." Telford's fee was five guineas a day—a high rate in Sweden at that time. Telford accepted Thunberg's scheme to a large extent, though he altered the line in many places and recommended locks of greater size and number.

In 1809, the year after Telford's visit, came the bloodless revolution when the new Constitution was adopted at the Diet of that year. At the same Diet State support for the proposed canal was voted. In 1810 Napoleon's Marshal Bernadotte, who was to be crowned Charles XIV of Sweden, was elected Crown Prince and soon became the virtual leader of the country. He strongly and immediately supported Platen in his canal plans and, indeed, regarded the Count as an indispensable general adviser.

In that same year of 1809 a set of beautiful hand-coloured maps of the

60

proposed canal (now preserved at the Canal Company's offices at Motala) were prepared by four of Platen's assistants and all bore the copied signature "Thos. Telford, Sept. 1808." On these maps New Towns were drawn in at four places—towns which Platen was certain would grow up as a result of the canal's existence; in the end only Motala achieved the status of a town. These maps, together with a translation of Telford's report, were presented to the Riksdag and in 1810 the Canal Company was formed, four days after men of the Östgöta Grenadiers had begun digging at Motala. Shares were over-subscribed by 100 per cent. Everything looked promising in that brief period of boom.

In spite of several reminders from Platen, Telford seems never to have sent a full sheet of costs but eventually he gave a rough estimate of £400,000. In the end the cost was more than five times the estimate. The time the canal would take to build was estimated at 10 years at the outside; in the end the time taken was 22 years.

Because of the extra cost and the slowness of the work, Platen was compelled to fight many long and bitter battles in the Diets. At one point, indeed, he nearly gave up the struggle in despair. But at long last the canal was completed, three years after Platen's death. It had been a tremendous undertaking for so small and poor a country; it had been initiated at a time of revolution and built during one of the most stringent periods in Swedish history a period of rapid inflation and financial instability—and in earlier years a period of international tensions and war as well.

The building of the canal was not merely a matter of digging the ditch itself but of blasting through many a granite rock ("rock blowing" as Platen called it), of constructing 58 locks, 35 bridges, 27 culverts and three dry docks, and of erecting demountable timber barracks for the thousands of infantrymen and their officers who were employed on the works, as well as houses for administrative staff, hospitals, stores, cook-houses, bakeries, stables, barges, pumps, cranes and so on. Over 80 million man-hours were required to dig away over 200 million cubic feet of earth, to blast away seven million cubic feet of rock and lay nearly nine million cubic feet of masonry.

And in the end the Blue Ribbon of Sweden was not the financial success that had been expected. In 1857 the tolls at the Sound were removed, the railways came as serious competitors in the sixties and finally the military value of the canal declined. Nevertheless the canal has acted since its completion as a useful alternative means of communication across the country, not least as a popular route for summer tourists. The Canal Company is now virtually owned by Stockholms Enskilda Bank and the Company maintains the canal in good condition, being content to lose money on it each year because by owning the canal it receives adequate compensation from the forest concessions owned by the Company. Both the Trollhätte Canal and the Södertälje Canal are now state-owned.

Regarded in realistic, and not purely monetary terms, the Göta Canal has always been and remains a national asset. Since a Royal Commission on waterways sat in Sweden between 1916 and 1922, there has been some talk about carrying out the recommendations by increasing the size of the Göta Canal and by decreasing the number of its locks and bridges, but so far nothing has been done and the canal retains to this day its early nineteenth-century style, size and charm—perhaps an advantage to tourists if not to trade.

THE TELFORD-PLATEN CORRESPONDENCE

The story of how the canal was built is vividly presented in the letters which were exchanged between Telford and Platen during the 20 or so years during which the canal was building. The correspondence is interesting, full of human touches, especially so the letters of Platen which are more outspoken, far longer and more numerous than the terse, factual, somewhat impersonal, though always courteous, letters of Telford, who never wasted his energy, not even on a needless word.

Platen invites Telford to visit Sweden and give his advice on the proposed canal. On June 1808 Telford replies from Inverness:—

> "I am particularly desirous of affording every assistance in my power to the accomplishing so noble and useful a Work and no trifling obstacles or inconvenience shall stand in the way."

Telford then travels to Sweden in a British man-of-war, the northern seas being infested at that time by Danish and French privateers. Having accomplished his survey, written his report and made friends for life of Platen and his wife, he boards a ship at the beginning of October at Gothenburg for the journey home. From Gothenburg Platen sends a letter to the ship which is held up by bad weather. The letter is typical in its lively, fluent style of improvised English and reveals the growing respect and affection the patrician feels towards the Scottish crofter's son. It concludes:—

> "Lastly You see mankind are always so foolish either to run away from or run after each other now as in the biginning running away would not do for our business we soon found since that it would not do neither for our affections; and that the reason why I now find myself always in the habitude of running or looking after You.

62

LEFT, *a contemporary record of the building of the locks at Heda about the year 1830 from a painting by A. C. Wetterling in the National Museum, Stockholm. Among the group of V. I. P:s can be seen Charles XIV (Napoleon's former Marshal, Jean Bernadotte) talking to his adviser, Count Baltzar von Platen. Above them in the distance is Vreta Church and far off on the horizon lies the city of Linköping.*

RIGHT, *another contemporary record, this time of the construction of the Trollhätte Canal, drawn by the French artist Louis Joseph Ange Cordier de Bonneville, who planned but never completed a large picture-book about Sweden.*

"Well make of it what you can but I think if tomorrow morning there is a fresh westerly wind You may as well come a shore once more for to fetch a bettre wind, seamans always do this and find it answer very well."

For the first four years all seems to have gone well with the operations in spite of lack of trained overseers and workmen, perhaps because most of the work then consisted in digging. In 1811, 5,000 men were employed, the bulk being Swedish infantrymen working a twelve-hour day; there were also a few hundred lay workers and some 150 Russian captives "that have deserted on the road home being tired of their despotic government" as Major Bagge, the engineer in charge, described them.

In 1813 Telford paid his second and last visit to Sweden to inspect work in progress. That year the first two British workmen were sent over by Telford, namely James Simpson and John Wilson. The next year five more followed—James Smith, David Lyon, William Urquhart, Alexander McKenzie and Alexander Fraser. At the same time two promising young Swedish lieutenants, J. Edström and G. Lagerheim, were sent to England at the Canal Company's expense to gain experience for nine months under Telford. In later years other British masons and craftsmen were to go to Sweden; in 1817, for example, 13 were being employed. Their wages varied from £70 a year to more than £200, plus travelling and living expenses, which must have been very good pay in those days. Many of these men were Scottish and Platen preferred them to others, for, as he wrote to Telford on one occasion, he found them "easier conforming to the people and country." But whoever they were, Platen seems to have treated them all very well, acting towards them, as one employee wrote home, "as a father and friend."

In the year 1814 Sweden was at war with Norway, but after that there was peace. The troubles on the canal henceforth were to be mainly financial. 1815 was the critical year in which Platen nearly resigned from the Canal Company. He wrote on 27 August:—

"Peace and the union of Norway performed, a Diet was the consequence of this; and having found by the calculations made at the end of the last year that the funds of the Company by no means were adequate to the work as yet to be performed . . . I published the bad news in the middle of March, the Diet having been assembled a fortnight! What a damned noise! what an outcry! All the sence and nonsense of the whole Country at once in motion . . . All sort of reproaches from all sides were merciless thrown out and till beginning of August I have mostly alone been standing in Butt in the House of Nobles! A fine and pleasing occupation when we think ourself actuatet only by seale for common welfar! . . . Damn them all they have embittered a whole Summer to me . . ."

In 1817 Platen decided that, in order to save the great expense of importing foreign products, he must establish a factory in Sweden that would make iron bridges, lock gates and so on for his canal in preference to more temporary works of timber; later on he hoped also to make and repair steam engines there. Eventually the Canal Company did build an iron works at Motala under the direction of an able Scot, Daniel Fraser, who now lies buried in Motala churchyard. The works proved their value but financial difficulties arose and in 1840 they were sold to a private company. Today those works, known as Motala Verkstad, are among the most important industrial concerns in the country; the trim white passenger steamers which make their delectable journeys in summer time along the canal have mostly been made there.

1822 was an eventful year. In the spring Platen visited Telford in England and made a five-weeks' tour with him, inspecting the numerous works of the engineer then in progress. In September the Western Line through Västergötland was opened with great ceremony and Lakes Vänern and Vättern were joined at last. A banquet at Hajstorp was given for 200 guests when Charles XIV honoured Platen and gave to the British workmen and overseers gold medals struck for the occasion.

There were delays on the Eastern Line during 1823, and 1824 was in some ways the worst year in the canal's building, mainly on account of costly troubles on Lake Viken where dangerous underwater rocks in the fairway had to be blasted away and where the dam had to be entirely rebuilt. But Platen pressed on.

In 1827, before the Diet had adjourned, Platen was sent to Christiania as Viceroy with the commission of trying to save the tottering Union. Like Telford he was now ageing and tired.

After a fortnight's illness, apparently internal cancer, Platen died in Christiania in December 1829. An extract from Platen's last letter to Telford written in Christiania, 18 May 1829, reads with the pathos of a rather weary old man: "I have done my duty tho' with little gratitude." But at least he died in the knowledge that his life's purpose would soon be accomplished. He lies buried beneath a great, unwrought monolith of granite on the bank of his beloved canal at Motala at a site he had himself

RIGHT, *the beautifully engraved share certificate, issued by the Göta Canal Company in May 1810.*

Legman Ollingren

No   4759

Till utförande af Götha Canal, har Innehafvaren tecknat
Sig för ett Capital af Ett Hundrade Riksdaler som á Ett
Hundrade Riksdaler per Actie utgör 1. Actier, hvarpå
dels vid Anteckningen, dels vid Actiens emottagande är betalt 10 Procent. eller 10 Rd. Och försäkras Innehafvaren, att under de villkor
Kongl. Majts den 11 April för Götha Canal Bolag i
Nåder utfärdade Octroy, Discont Reglemente och Bolags Reglor inne-
hålla, uti Bolaget och Deß Discont werk, samt alla öfriga Bolaget Nå-
digst förunte förmäner och rättigheter, vara delaglig i mon af den tecknade
Summan, samt således för alt hvad deraf kan utbetalas njuta Fem Procent
årligen under Byggnadstiden, med den tillökning sedermera, som Canal
och Discont werkens inkomster medgifva, samt Discont Reglementet
och Bolags Reglorne omständeligare förmäla, börandes vid alla Ut-
delningar Original Actierne uppvisas och påskrifvas

Stockholm den 28 May 1810.

Riksdaler 100.   Banco,   Fol. 149

På Götha Canal Bolags vägnar

Hagerheim   M Wennblm   B. v. Platen

Carl Arfwedson   B H Santesson

Ollingren

På Ofvanstäende Actier är betalt

1611

April d. 1. Ytterligare 15 Procent med   1815.

M Helsingius

Ollingren

LEFT, *the King's Grotto (a giant's kettle) at Trollhättan, formed in the rock during the Ice Age. Therein a number of kings have had their names inscribed on visits to the Falls.*

LEFT, *one of the old, disused locks at Trollhättan.*

The *Göta Canal near Norsholm and one of its early rolling bridges of iron.*

RIGHT, *the post of a lock gate on the canal (photos by* ERIC DE MARÉ*).*

A lithograph of Nils Ericson, who worked on the construction of canal in his youth and later became a famous railway engineer. His brother John, who also worked on the canal, later achieved fame in America as an engineer.

selected. Since that stone was laid the debt of gratitude has been amply repaid by his countrymen.

The Eastern Line through Östergötland from Motala to Mem was opened on 26 September 1832, nearly three years after Platen's death. Again Charles XIV, now 68 years old, performed the ceremony, accompanied this time by the Queen and by his son, the Crown Prince, and his wife. At Söderköping the King went aboard the royal yacht *Esplendian* which sailed to Mem and passed through the last lock into the Baltic Sea. The ceremonies of the day concluded with a grand feast at Mem to symbolise in rejoicing the fact that the old dream had now come true and that the two seas were at last united.

THE STORY OF THE CANAL SINCE ITS OPENING

The Göta Canal between Sjötorp and Mem remains much the same today as it was when it was completed and so it retains the charm of the early engineering period. But later developments have taken place on the rest of the navigation between Gothenburg and Stockholm. The short link between the Baltic and Lake Mälaren—the Södertälje Canal—was rebuilt to somewhat larger dimensions than the Göta Canal in 1819 and was again enlarged in 1924. Towards the end of 1822, the year the Western Line of the Göta Canal was opened, Platen surveyed the River Göta and the Trollhätte Canal with a view to improving the navigation between Gothenburg and Lake Vänern, the locks there being smaller than those that had been built on the Göta Canal. New locks were finally opened on the Trollhätte Canal in 1844 and this produced more traffic on the Göta Canal itself. This work was under the direction of Nils Ericson (1802-70) who had served his apprenticeship under Platen on the Göta Canal works as a boy, together with his more famous brother, John Ericsson (1803-89), inventor of the first practicable screw propeller and of the revolving gun turret. Nils later became an important railway engineer in Sweden while his brother John emigrated to America in 1839 where he lived for the rest of his life and where he established himself as a designer of iron ships, including the renowned *Monitor*.

Between 1909 and 1916 the Trollhätte Canal under the engineer F. V. Hansen was again enlarged and obtained very much bigger locks than those on the Göta Canal, locks measuring 295 feet long and 50 feet wide. The bottle-neck is now therefore on the Göta Canal.

The traffic on the Göta Canal since its opening has, of course, been mainly commercial and during the nineteenth century most of the mercantile vessels were schooners which hoisted their sails across the lakes and in the narrow cuts too, no doubt, when the wind was favourable, but which were

71

drawn along by horses or oxen treading the towpaths when the wind was unfavourable. Indeed, draft oxen were being used right up to the years of the First World War. Today many fine schooners, some a century old, though now fitted with modern diesel engines, still trade along the canal. Large modern motor vessels can also be seen, such as those owned by the *Vieille Montagne*, a Belgian company which mines zinc ore at Åmmeberg to the north of Lake Vättern and transports it along the canal to Gothenburg where it is transhipped to Belgium. Many other craft also ply the waterway today carrying up to 250 tons each. When travelling along the canal you will pass a great variety of vessels, anything from a new oil tanker to a noble old schooner, from a sleek, rich yacht to a collapsible canoe. On an average 10 or 12 boats of different kinds will pass each lock on a summer day. Between about mid-December and mid-April frost sets in and the canal is closed to all navigation.

Since its opening the canal has consistently carried grain, timber, pitprops and firewood, coal and coke, various ores, limestone, marble, salt, herring, pig and scrap iron, worked iron and steel. Other freight includes foodstuffs of all kinds, tar, wood pulp, paper, matches, chemicals, asphalt, cement, glass, porcelain, tiles and bricks, copper, machinery and many other things besides. In 1870 the vessels, both sail and steam, using the canal numbered 2,715. In 1939 the number was 5,273. In 1951 it had dropped to 2,912—a sad comment on the effects of the Second World War and on the increasing competition of road transport. In latter years, however, the traffic has increased and it is clear that the canal, even in its present condition, will perform a valuable job for a long time to come.

Contrary to some opinions, transport on inland waterways is not an out-of-date method, as the flourishing and developing waterways of the Continent reveal. But if waterways are to keep their position they must be made as efficient as possible. It is to be hoped that the recommendations of the Swedish Canal Commission of 1916-1922 (or even better ones) will eventually be applied to the Göta Canal so that the cross-country journey can be speedier and be accomplished by sea-going vessels as large as those which now use the Trollhätte Canal. If the locks on the Göta Canal were enlarged, the number of movable bridges reduced, the winding cut straightened here and there and perhaps another cut made between Lake Roxen and Lake Glan and thence past Norrköping into the arm of the Baltic called Bråviken, the commercial traffic on the canal could be greatly increased and sea-going ships could use the whole waterway from Gothenburg and Stockholm. This would reduce handling at the ports; for instance, the zinc ore from Åmmeberg could be carried all the way to Belgium in the same ships instead of being re-shipped at Gothenburg as it is at present. The first step in such a project should be the enlargement of the

The ceremonial opening of the Östgöta Line of the Göta Canal at Mem in 1832 from a painting of 1855 by J. Chr. Berger, now in the Östergötland Museum, Linköping. King Charles XIV can be seen in the bows of his yacht Esplendian acknowledging the ovations of the crowd.

Western Line joining Lakes Vänern and Vättern, because Vättern, Sweden's second largest lake, has a considerable population and a number of important industrial centres around its shores which would benefit by a larger outlet to the sea.

It is significant that in 1960 the tonnage passing through the Trollhätte Canal was over three million whereas the tonnage on the Göta Canal in that year was less than a quarter of a million. Those three million tons, incidentally, would require the use of 600 extra railway waggons per day if the Trollhätte Canal did not exist. That the Göta Canal has not paid its way since the Second World War does not indicate that it is an anachronism; we are too easily blinded these days by the mere figures of cost accountancy. Considered in terms of real wealth, waterway transport is by far the most economical means of transport, for the simple, basic reason that movement through water produces very little friction; whereas one horse can move two tons on a level road, and 10 tons on rail, it can move as much as 80 tons on water. Apart from that factor, canals have other assets than the single one of commercial transport: they help land drainage, they can act as water conservators and distributors, they form pleasant landscape features, they help to preserve wild life and they provide healthy pleasure grounds for fishing, boating and tourism. Thus they cannot be regarded in a national sense only as commercial transport arteries.

THE CANAL AS A TOURIST ROUTE

As a tourist route the Göta Canal has been important since its inauguration and is now world-renowned. As such it provides Sweden not only with foreign currency but also with extra-national goodwill. Indeed, those who use it for pleasure during the summer season are today mostly tourists from abroad, especially American-Swedes. The Göta Canal Steamship Company, which alone runs passenger steamers on the canal, is now almost a national institution for it was founded way back in 1869. But as early as 1826, even before the canal was complete, the paddle steamer *Braut Anund* voyaged from Gothenburg and along the Västgöta Line nearly to Linköping. In 1834 the *Amiral von Platen* voyaged the whole way from Stockholm to Gothenburg and that was the real start of the passenger traffic on the canal. That ship was a fiddle-form paddle steamer having a plan shaped like a violin so that it bulged outwards both fore and aft of each paddle, thus providing the maximum width which would pass through the locks.

In those early days the journey between Gothenburg and Stockholm took from four to five days because the vessels did not move at night. Life was more leisurely then. At evening when the steamer was snugly moored the time would be passed pleasantly in games and dancing by both passengers and crew. A member of the crew would stroll along the towpath playing a violin while others followed stopping at the locks to fill or empty them in readiness for the next day's journey.

With the coming of the screw propeller in the 1840:ies things were much improved because the whole of each vessel could then be as wide as the locks. Further improvement came in 1844 when the locks on the Troll-hätte Canal were rebuilt to the same width as those on the Göta Canal. Today two of the passenger vessels—*Wilhelm Tham* and *Diana*—are still driven by steam; they are not equipped with modern diesels for the reasons that, first, speed along the canal reaches is limited to less than five knots so that powerful engines are not required and, secondly, that steam engines are much quieter than diesels and produce less vibration; in fact their gentle hissing and throbbing soothe one to sleep at nights and do not disturb the bucolic peace of the lovely waterway. Those three steamers now carry about 6,000 travellers each summer season, half of these being cabin passengers and half deck passengers.

For the past 80 years over a million people have travelled on the passenger steamers between Gothenburg and Stockholm—a remarkably mixed cross-section of humanity of all nations, classes and professions— kings and peasants, aristocrats and business men, priests and diplomats, artists and artisans, maharajas and writers. Among the writers, Sven Hedin, Henrik Ibsen, Hans Chr. Andersen, Jane Wilde (Oscar Wilde's mother who wrote poetry under the pen-name of *Speranza*), H. G. Wells and Jean-Paul Sartre have made the canal trip and most of them have somewhere recorded their impressions of the journey in the written word. The distinguished Swedish actor Anders de Wahl travelled on the *Pallas* as a young man in the year 1891 with the contract for his first professional part in his pocket. Of this, his first, journey he has written with typical enthusiasm:

"The voyage became one long party. We sat round a long table on the top deck and sang duets and quartets. I would often think during the few hours of darkness of the summer nights, when I would steal away from the beauty gliding by and listen down below to the slow and soothing beat of the engine, that if this my first journey into the world was a symbol of my future journey through life, then, by Heaven, I might indeed be filled with confidence."

RIGHT, *the locks at Trollhättan depicted in a lithograph by the Frenchman Eugène Ciceri, one of a number of illustrations in "Voyage en Scandinavie," published by A. F. Mayer in the 1840:ies. The Göta Canal when completed stimulated a flowering of such picturesque travel-books, which charmingly illustrated the landscapes of the waterway. Other examples follow.*

The mount of Kinnekulle rising above the Westgothian plain. A lithograph from a drawing by F. C. Kiærschou from "Sverige framställdt i taflor" (1850-56).

The Canal at Borenshult, a lithograph from a drawing by F. C. Kiærschou from "Sverige framställdt i taflor" (1850-56).

The Canal near Söderköping drawn by C. J. Billmark and lithographed by C. Cardon in "Från Stockholm till Göteborg. Pittoreska Vyer från Göta Kanal och dess närheter."

Läckö Castle by C. J. Billmark, one of the lithographs from "Pittoresk resetour från Stockholm till Neapel" (1852).

SUBSIDIARY NAVIGATIONS

For the information of amateur yachtsmen who like to explore fresh waters in the depths of the countryside and have the time to extend their journey across Sweden, the following three navigations which link up with the Göta Canal cross-country waterway are worth considering. All of them are, unfortunately, dead-end navigations, but all possess beautiful scenery. On some of them journeys can be made regular by passenger vessels.

Dalsland Canal: This is perhaps Sweden's most beautiful waterway. It begins at Köpmannebro on the west coast of Lake Vänern and runs for many miles north-north-west up to the Norwegian border. It is 160 miles long of which only five miles are man-made cuts, the depth in these cuts being 5 feet 9 inches. The rest of the waterway consists of a series of long and narrow lakes. It has 29 locks in all.

Säffle Canal: This also begins on the west coast of Lake Vänern but some miles north of Köpmannebro near Säffle. It extends more or less due north up to Arvika on the Glafsfjord in Värmland. The navigation is about 56 miles long and is again mainly a chain of long, narrow lakes or fjords, the artificial cuts being only about eight miles in all. The difference in level from the northern end to Lake Vänern is no more than three feet so that no locking is required. At its southern part it can pass vessels of 11 feet draught.

Kinda Canal runs due south from Lake Roxen in Östergötland through Linköping right down to Horn near the Småland border, a distance of about 50 miles. The navigation is mainly composed of River Stångån and the lakes Erlången, Lilla and Stora Rängen, Järnlunden and Åsunden. There are 15 locks, the minimum depth for navigation being five feet. The short distance between Lake Roxen and Linköping's dock is built in conformity with the Göta Canal. This short distance up to Linköping is still used by

LEFT, *at Håverud, an aqueduct in the form of a huge steel trough carries the Dalsland Canal across a river while a viaduct carries a railway across the canal.*

79

commercial craft but the rest of the navigation is now used only by one tourist passenger steamer. This is also a lovely waterway and deserves the patronage of small pleasure craft. Most of the country through which it passes is sparsely inhabited and provides a refreshing sense of remoteness; here and there rises a fine old mansion, such as that at Sturefors, or some fantastic baroque spire such as that of the church at Horn.

Three Other Navigations link up with the cross-country artery and all three run into Lake Mälaren. Again they are dead-end navigations. To the far west of Mälaren lies the Arboga River and some miles up that river the *Hjälmare Canal*—one having the longest history of all canals in the country—runs southwards into Lake Hjälmaren. At the western end of that lake lies the large industrial town of Örebro.

Strömsholms Canal, going northwards from the west end of Mälaren, is a more beautiful navigation and is available for vessels of no more than 5 feet 3 inches draught. It was first built between 1777 and 1795, and was for a time a commercial route for iron ore. Its length is about 67 miles and it reaches right into the province of Dalarna. Before deciding to explore this waterway, amateur yachtsmen should ascertain the minimum height of bridges because some of these have recently been rebuilt as fixed structures.

The third of the navigations running into Mälaren is the series of lakes and sounds lying between the Görväln inlet just west of Stockholm and Graneberg just south of Uppsala. On the way lies the charming old town of Sigtuna. This is a popular summer tourist route for passenger steamers from Stockholm.

A BRANCH JOURNEY

An old summer tourist route connected with the Göta Canal may interest those who are free to travel where they wish in their own craft and who want to break their cross-country journey in order to see more of Sweden than is possible on the direct voyage between Gothenburg and Stockholm. This is the Berg to Jönköping route. If you travel this route, you should call both at Vadstena and at the fascinating island of Visingsö. Various combined tours are possible. For example, one may travel to Jönköping by bus or train from Gothenburg, then by boat to Vadstena and tranship there to one of the Göta Canal steamers bound either for Stockholm or Gothenburg. Alternatively the whole route from Jönköping to Berg may be taken: then Vreta Monastery may be thoroughly seen and Linköping also with its famous Gothic cathedral and its Museum. From Linköping, of course, trains and buses run to Stockholm or Gothenburg.

Visingsö is certainly worth visiting. Vättern's only sizeable island, it is

ABOVE, *a lock on the Kinda Canal.* BELOW, *the manor of Sturefors, built about 1700, can be seen from this waterway (photos by* ERIC DE MARÉ).

eight-and-a-half miles long and one-and-a-half miles wide, yet it is rich in historical monuments and the creations of past centuries and cultures. It was a military stronghold in medieval days and after. It has been inhabited, however, for at least 4,000 years, as the ancient graves which have been discovered on the island reveal. It is best known for its many associations with the powerful Brahe family which at one time owned large tracts of Småland and Västergötland.

Count Per Brahe the Elder began to build the castle of Visingsborg in the 1560:ies and Per Brahe the Younger, who became Governor of Finland, completed it in the following century and even set up his own government on the island, so big a fellow was he. Unfortunately the castle is now a ruin, having been burned down in 1718, probably by Russian prisoners of war captured by the army of Charles XII.

The most interesting building on this delightful little island, with its flourishing mulberry trees and its mild climate, is the Brahe Church near Visingsborg built in 1636 as the family chapel of the Brahes. It has been well restored and contains many objects of interest and beauty.

LEFT, *a passenger ship enters a lock (Brokind) on the Kinda Canal, which runs into Lake Roxen at Linköping. The trip from Linköping to Rimforsa takes seven hours, and to Horn nine-and-a-half hours.* ABOVE, *the town of Vänersborg. From an old wood engraving.*

AMATEUR YACHTSMEN ON THE CANAL

The journey across Sweden by water is described in this book mainly for those who travel on the passenger steamers. But the book should also serve those who travel the canal in their own small craft. For them a brief chapter of information and advice on navigation is now provided.

The highest permissible speed in the Göta Canal itself is 4.8 knots but along the dam or guiding wall in Lake Viken and when passing through Brosundet, the narrow strait in Lake Viken north-west of Forsvik, speed must be reduced to a maximum of four knots.

The greatest permissible length of vessels on the Göta Canal is 32 meters (105 feet), greatest beam is 7 meters (23 feet) and greatest draught is 2.82 meters (9 feet 3 inches). The figures for the Trollhätte Canal are 286 : : 41 : 14.9 feet and for the Södertälje Canal 396 : 60 : 18 feet.

Anchoring a vessel or punting it in the canal is prohibited; nor may one bathe, fish or shoot there. Bathing in the lakes is, of course, a different matter.

A vessel may not be moored between a red-white pole and a lock or bridge. Where the canal runs through the narrow passage between rocks just west of Lake Viken—that is between Lanthöjden and Tåtorp—nine meeting places are provided and are indicated by notice boards on the northern or eastern bank. Take care in this narrow passage because a large motor vessel cannot be stopped suddenly by foot brakes; it may bear down on you remorselessly and you may have no room to pass on either side.

RIGHT, *a private motor-boat locks up on the Göta Canal at Berg in Östergöt-land. "The transit across Sweden occupies three days, progress being slow, owing to the number of locks and the tortuous navigation through the abrupt curves and undulations of the canal. But the excursion never wearies. There is a rich and interesting country around, and a rest at every town for loading an unloading, which gives ample time to land and investigate the buildings and the people" (Lady* JANE FRANCESCA WILDE *in "Driftwood from Scandinavia", 1884).*

84

TOP LEFT, *a private motorboat enters a lock at Berg.*

TOP CENTRE, *a lock at Trollhättan, whose huge steel gates are operated by electricity.*

TOP RIGHT, *a sumptuous English yacht enters a lock at Sjötorp.*

RIGHT, *a member of the crew of a Göta Canal steamer turns a lock paddle at Motala (photos by* ERIC DE MARÉ).

LEFT, *two of sixteen sulphite boilers made at a Karlstad factory being floated along the Göta Canal on their journey to Russia—evidence of the continuing viability of the old canal as a commercial route (photo* JAN OLOV MAGNUSSON).

Evening settles over Lake Viken near the summit level of the Göta Canal.

As for precedence, when vessels arrive at a lock or bridge, a passenger steamer has right of way over commercial craft. Pleasure craft, however, should give way to all vessels in regular canal service and may be directed to make a brief stop in order to await the arrival of other small craft so that all can make a simultaneous passage through a lock or flight of locks. If in doubt, follow the instructions of the lock-keeper.

SIGNALS

Sound Signals: A long blast is an attention-and-reply signal for eastbound vessels. Two long blasts are for westbound vessels. A short blast followed by a long one indicates "I am proceeding." A long one followed by a short indicates "I have stopped." The attention-and-reply signal is given:—

(a) Before arrival at a narrow section or where visibility is bad. (In the case of two vessels arriving at a narrow passage where passing is impossible the latest to arrive shall wait).

(b) At meeting at night when the intention is to pass a vessel ahead (in which case the vessel ahead shall give a reply signal, slow down and keep to one side).

(c) When a vessel approaches a bridge or lock (at night this should produce an illumination on lock or bridge).

(d) When an eastbound vessel is leaving Motala Lock and when a westbound vessel is passing Platen's Grave east of Motala bridges and lock.

Special Sound Signals: Near Forsvik lie several very narrow channels and sharp bends. Here special signals are given and the amateur yachtsman is advised to know what they mean. They are:—

Just before entering	GIVEN BY	
	Eastbound vessels	Westbound vessels
Spetsnäs Canal (1,700 meters west of Forsvik)	—	— — —
Bilströmmen (west of Forsvik)	— — •	— —
Forsvik Canal	• • •	—

When arriving at Rödesund, the short sound between Lakes Botten and Vättern, and also when arriving at Motala harbour from Lake Vättern, the following signals are given:—

For passing through the bridge and lock   —   —   —

For mooring at the quay   —

Visual Signals and Warnings: A diagonally-placed white board gives the warning that you will reach a bridge or lock 300 meters further on. A whistle signal—one for eastbound and two for westbound vessels—and in some cases the showing of a green screen, flag or light is a signal to proceed. A red screen, flag or light is a warning that the way is not clear.

Semaphore signals exist at two places: (i) At Tåtorp Lock west of Lake Viken for the narrow, rocky section of canal west of Tåtorp and (ii) at Forsvik Lock for the Forsvik Canal. These semaphores are fitted with two adjustable vanes and a lantern showing white, red or green lights. They give the following signals in reply to the sound signals of a vessel:— If the vane to the left of the column points obliquely upwards at 45 degrees, or if a green light shows, the passage is clear. If the same vane points horizontally, or a red light shows, the passage is not clear.

LOCKING

When a vessel enters a lock the greatest care should be taken not to ram the front gates. Inside the lock the vessel should be moored to the bollards and if possible the propeller should be stopped. If locking down, the rudder must clear the stone sill and should be laid hard over away from the mooring side. The crew of the vessel must attend to the mooring and the owner is responsible for any damage caused to locks by lack of proper attention to this. Passage through locks is under the direction of the lock-keeper but the owner and crew are expected to assist him in mooring the vessel, raising and lowering the sluices on the lock gates and in opening or closing the gates. Letting water in or out by turning the wheels which lift the sluices must not be commenced until the lock-keeper whistles a signal.

Small pleasure craft can be badly damaged in locks without proper procedure. Here is the correct procedure when locking down. One of the crew jumps ashore just above the lock with mooring rope in hand; boat enters lock gently on its motor or else the shore crew hauls the boat into the lock. Lock-keeper closes the upper gates and lets down the paddles or sluices. Shore crew hangs on to mooring rope, helmsman turns rudder hard over, jumps ashore and runs to front gates where, on hearing the whistle from the lock-keeper, starts to wind up the paddles; that is quite hard work.

Locking up is more tricky. One member of crew jumps ashore to starboard just below lock with mooring rope; helmsman steers vessel in to starboard side of lock. Shore crew takes two turns with rope round a bollard well to front end of lock and goes back to close one of lower gates while

ABOVE, *passengers relax on the deck of a minor Göta Canal steamer, while,* RIGHT, *officers share a joke on the bridge.*

lock-keeper closes the other. Shore crew now runs to front gates and of the four sluice wheels he chooses the second one from the starboard and turns this with discretion judging the amount to raise the sluice according to the rush of water into the lock and the size of the vessel. When the first sluice is fully wound up, the shore crew works the first paddle to starboard (the right), and then the one to port (extreme left) and finally the one on the middle left. This last one should be lifted slowly. If this method is adopted the craft will ride easily as she is lifted up and no buffeting will occur.

Small boats will require plenty of fenders when locking through and large yachts should have their sides well protected with sacks of straw which can be acquired at Sjötorp or at Mem at the termini of the Göta Canal. The large electric locks on the Trollhätte and Södertälje Canals are, surprisingly enough, far easier to deal with than the smaller hand-worked locks on the Göta Canal proper because the entrance of the water there is regulated mechanically with great sensitivity and precision.

TOLLS

Main canal offices of the Göta Canal proper, where tolls can be paid, are situated at Sjötorp, Motala and Mem. Tolls for the Trollhätte Canal can be paid at Trollhättan and for the Södertälje Canal at the single canal lock there.

If pleasure craft wish to travel by night—that is between 10 p. m. and 6 a. m.—a special night fee is charged which must be paid to the lock-keepers and bridge-keepers. At solitary bridges the money is placed in a bag extended by the keeper as the boat passes through the bridge hole.

The locks at Åkersberg. From an old wood engraving.

93

A canal passenger boat leaves Gothenburg (photo by THE GÖTA CANAL STEAM-SHIP COMPANY).

THE JOURNEY

*M*ap *of the middle part of Sweden with the canal route between Gothenburg and Stockholm. Passenger steamers start the journey in either direction between Gothenburg and Stockholm on three days of each week from the end of May until the beginning of September. On one day of the week on the westbound journey the steamer makes a detour south to take in Lidköping and also, if weather permits, Läckö Castle; this adds five hours to the normal time of about 58 hours. Time tables for the whole journey are shown on pages 109-110. The journey is 347 miles long, and 65 locks on the route raise vessels 304 feet above sea level to the sum-*

Fagersta · 16° · Heby · Gamla Uppsala · UPPSALA · Erken · Arho
Sala · Ultuna · Uppsala · Rimbo · Norrtälje
VÄSTMANLANDS LÄN · Skökloster · STOCKHOLMS · Furusund
iddarhyttan · Ramnäs · Skultuna · UPPLAND · Ångsö nat. park
TMANLAND · Surahammar · Tillberga · Enköping · LÄN · Sigtuna · Lindholmen · Ljusterö
sberg · Hallstahammar · Svartån · Sundbyberg · Danderyd · Täby · Möja
Nora · Frövi · Västerås · Solna · Djursholm · Vaxholm · Grön
Än · Köping · M a l a r e n · Sundbyberg · Lidingö · Sändha
nat. park · Kungsör · Torshälla · STOCKHOLM · Nacka · Alm
Örebro · Arboga · Strängnäs · Gripsholm · Saltsjöbaden
Hjälmaren · Eskilstuna · Mariefred · Rönninge · SÖDERTÄLJE · LÄN · Dalarö
Kvarntorp · Rekarne · SÖDERMANLANDS · Huddinge · Ömö
nla · Pålsboda · Vingåker · SÖDERMANLAND · SÖDERTÖRN · Dalarö
rg · Sottern · Flen · Sparreholm · Muskö · Huvudskär
ÄRKE · Ammeberg · Katrineholm · Valla · Båven · Gnesta · St. Vika · Utö
Rejmyra · Yngaren · LÄN · Vagnhärad · Trosa · Nynäshamn
ammar · Tylösko · Finspång · Åby · Kolmården · Nyköping · Landsort
Boren · Glan · Bråviken · OXELÖSUND · Havringe · ·459
ÖSTERGÖTLANDS · Norrköping · Vikbolandet · Arkösund
BERG · Roxen · Mariefred · nat. pa
Skänninge · Linköping · SÖDERKÖPING
ÖSTERGÖTLAND · Bjärka-Säby · Gusum · Harstena
LÄN · Mjölby · Ålvidaberg · Valdemarsvik · Häradskär
Boxholm · Rimforsa · Fd · Överum
Sommen · Åsunden · Kappelshamn · Lär
IGE · Kisa · Horn · Gamleby · Storkläppen · Tingstäde · Sm
Aneby · Österbymo · Gullringen · Södra Vi · Ankarsrum · Västervik · Visby
N. Kvills nat. park Stångån · Vimmerby · GOTLANDS · Roma klos
Eksjö · Mariannelund · LÄN · Tors
LÄN · Hultsfred · KALMAR · Klintehamn · GOTLA
dafors · Vetlanda · Målilla · Figeholm · Ölands · Karlsö L. · Ljug
norra udde · St

mit of the waterway at Lanthöjden and down again. The waterway from Gothenburg to Lake
Vänern, composed mainly of the Göta River, is called the Trollhätte Canal and is navigable
by large freighters. The old Platen-Telford cut—the Göta Canal proper— begins at Sjötorp,
on the eastern shore of Lake Vänern, its Västgöta Line running as far as Lake Vättern. The
Östgöta Line of the Canal runs from Motala to Mem on an arm of the Baltic Sea. The route
then runs through an archipelago, passes through the Södertälje Canal into Lake Mälaren and
thence eastward to Stockholm. — By courtesy of Generalstabens litografiska anstalt, Stockholm.

Gustav Adolfs Market Place, Gothenburg. The bronze statue of the king by Bengt Fogel-berg was erected in 1854. In the background is the Exchange.

GOTHENBURG

If you have the time and the means, stay a day or two in Gothenburg for it has a number of pleasures to offer its guests. Though the street vista along the Grand Canal (Stora Hamnkanalen) must be among the finest in Europe, most of the town's buildings are undistinguished. The general cachet of the place, however, is friendly, verdant and charming. For one thing Gothenburg is a large town but not larger than any town should be; with about 410,000 souls it can provide all the amenities of urban civilization and culture while still retaining a coherent form and entity. It is a city without the megalopolitan tensions—a city you can walk out of in a morning. Yet it is free from provincial stiffness and, being a large port, it has a lively cosmopolitan air and is in direct touch by sea with the rest of the world. Unlike many ports it is clean, tidy and unsqualid and the city fathers have watched over its growth and planning with care in the past so that hardly anywhere are you out of sight of trees. This is a maritime garden city of broad avenues, ubiquitous water and a system of parks and gardens which runs through the town as a brilliant, interpenetrating band of green.

THE TOWN'S CHARACTER

Most inhabitants of Gothenburg have at least some words of English, partly perhaps because the place has close links, both economic and cultural, with Great Britain—ties greatly strengthened by Napoleon's blockade of the Continent during the first decade of the nineteenth century when the port became the chief depot for British traders in northern Europe. The town is often called Little London and they say that when it rains in London the umbrellas go up in Gothenburg.

Gothenburg was built for trade, and today, with its ten miles of quays, it is essentially a carriers' centre and less of a mart than it was at one time. It also serves as the chief market for the West Coast fisheries and here are important ship-building yards and other industries. The whole place has an international air, not only because it is a port, but because it has been inhabited since its foundation by different races; first by Dutchmen, some of whom helped to build the town on a Dutch plan with fortifications, canals and moat. Immigrants were then encouraged and many German, Jewish, English and Scottish families came to settle here, some of whom founded large fortunes and established patrician lines. Among the Scots was Colin Campbell who was one of the founders of the Swedish East India Company. This established headquarters in Gothenburg in 1731 and greatly increased the town's importance. Some of the old Gothenburg families still flourish in the city and they have given much through the years to the community, for it became a tradition for those who became wealthy to help the town in some way—perhaps by the gift of a piece of parkland, a new hospital, a museum or a work of art. The place has always been a stronghold of liberalism and free trade in Scandinavia.

The author has thus tried to capture the atmosphere of Gothenburg in his book "Scandinavia":—

"Everything here is clean and orderly. The streets are lively and yet do not hold that nervous tension of the great continental capitals. The shop windows are filled with the best of wares and everyone looks well dressed. Bright signs project over the pavements and plenty of bunting is afloat. Cooling water streams down the plateglass windows of the charkuteri shops and in the restaurants proud waitresses in black and spotless white move with the dignity of countesses. The crowded narrow shopping streets gain intrigue by contrast with the broad park-lined avenues and with such wide spaces as that where the statue of Gothenburg's founder stands. You will notice the well-designed street furniture, the many neat konditori displaying rich pastries among the climbing plants, the ubiquity of fresh paint, sleek American cars and handsome young policemen who, in their white caps and gloves, swords swinging at their sides, give a gay, light-opera touch to the picture. The girls are pretty and soon we shall learn to distinguish a definite Gothenburg type with petite features, good complexion, straight back and, of course, blue eyes . . .

"In spite of having become a world port, Gothenburg is no Hot Spot of waterside brothels and night haunts, for the people are puritans all and take their leisure in a balanced bourgeois style. Even the Liseberg Amusement Park, owned and run by the municipality, is tidy and well-behaved with not a hair out of place—perhaps a little too prim . . . In the summer the pleasures of the skerries are near at hand—bathing, sailing, fishing . . . In the winter the cultural life is rich enough, for the town is renowned for the high standard of its music and drama . . . It is a Buddenbrooks kind of place."

100

HISTORY

Gothenburg was founded by Charles IX on the island of Hisingen, which lies at the mouth of the Göta River, but it was transferred to its present position in 1619 by Gustavus Adolphus who wanted to provide his country with a safe port in the west for trading outside the Baltic. With the help of Dutch experts the King laid out the town with a system of intersecting canals which would act not only as lanes of transport to the warehouses but would also act as land drains and as firebreaks. Some of these canals have now been filled in to become streets or parks. Initially the town was fortified with ramparts, forts and a moat and these were still existing up to 1820. Today a part of the moat remains as a pleasant zig-zag of water running through the central parkland, while the two outlying forts called Kronan and Göta Lejon still survive, the former now serving as a military museum.

Soon after its foundation, Gustavus Adolphus presented to the town one of its many parks—Slottsskogen to the south-west. Other parks have been added from time to time such as Keiller's Park on the island of Hisingen, Kungsparken in the centre which joins up with Trädgårdsföreningen's (Horticultural Society's) gardens, boasting a palm-house and a very good restaurant of Edwardian vintage.

During the present century the town has expanded enormously, yet the central market place—Gustav Adolfs Torg—retains its old character. From that market place a broad avenue runs southwards, up a slight slope and partly through parkland, to culminate in Götaplatsen, a *forum artis* laid out in 1923. This spinal column—Kungsportsavenyen usually referred to simply as The Avenue with its climax at Götaplatsen—gives firmness to the whole town plan and a sufficient degree of central monumentality. At the centre of Götaplatsen is *Poseidon*, one of Carl Milles' largest fountains, and around this are ranged the colonnaded Art Museum, a relic of the 1923 Exhibition, the City Theatre and the City Concert Hall. Of these buildings, the most distinguished by far is the Concert Hall designed by Nils Einar Eriksson and built in 1935—certainly one of the finest modern buildings in Sweden.

MUSEUMS

In the Art Museum may be seen the paintings, sculptures, etchings and other works of Sweden's most prominent artists, as well as pieces by foreign artists of repute—Rembrandt, Rubens, Van Dyck, Delacroix, Bonnard, Monet, Pissarro, Renoir, Courbet, Cézanne, Van Gogh, Munch, Matisse and others. It also contains a considerable collection of Scandinavian art.

Another collection worth visiting is the Röhss Museum, opened in 1916 and containing in its well-designed red brick building by Carl Westman a good collection of arts and crafts of the different periods, Swedish and foreign (including Japanese and Chinese objects). The Gothenburg Museum of Cultural History in the old East India Company's building in Norra Hamngatan by the Grand Canal, houses the most important of the town's collections, devoted to cultural history, ethnography and archaeology; it also includes a fine collection of the East India Company's porcelain imported from the Orient. The Natural History Museum in Slottsskogen and the Maritime Museum on the west side of Masthugget also contain good collections; the latter possesses an aquarium and many models and paintings of noted old ships. Incidentally, near the Maritime Museum rises the Seaman's Tower surmounted by a piece of sculpture, the Sailor's Wife, by Ivar Johnsson, and from the top of that tower a good view of the city and its harbour can be obtained.

NOTABLE BUILDINGS

Of the few old buildings of note we must mention the good classical building of the 1750:ies which was the East India Company's headquarters and now houses the Museum of Cultural History. The architects were well known in Sweden—Carl Hårleman and B. W. Carlberg. Just near that building stands Kristine kyrka (Christine Church) rebuilt in 1746; within are the monuments of a number of Scottish settlers in the town.

A few hundred yards to the east we come into the wide Gustav Adolfs Torg (market place) at the south-east corner of which stands the City Court House built in 1672 and restored in 1817 in a Palladian classicism. The most interesting part of the building, however, is the modern extension of 1937 by Gunnar Asplund, who was the leading architect of his generation in Sweden and was responsible also for such buildings as the City Library of Stockholm and the famous Stockholm Exhibition of 1930.

To the west of Lilla Torget (Little Market Place), which lies south of the Grand Canal, is the Lord Lieutenant's Residence built in 1648—50 for Marshal Lennart Torstensson, a fighter in the Thirty Years' War; there Charles X died in 1660. South of Lilla Torget, off Västra Hamngatan, stands the Cathedral facing a public garden which gives a sudden spacious release from the tightness of Kungsgatan. It hardly appears like a cathed-

RIGHT, *Gothenburg's main avenue seen from the Museum of Art across Göta-platsen, the city's forum artis, which is dominated by the great statue of Poseidon by Carl Milles—the city's maritime symbol.*

BELOW, *the Concert Hall of 1931, facing Götaplatsen, was designed by Nils Einar Ericsson.*
BELOW RIGHT, *the Gothenburg's Law Courts by Gunnar Asplund.*

LEFT, *the new Gothenburg Stadium, Nya Ullevi, holds 54,000 spectators.*

RIGHT, *the port of Gothenburg, the largest in Sweden. In 1963 the port handled a tonnage of over 16 million.*

ABOVE, *the centre of Norra Guldheden, Gothenburg, a modern residential area, planned as a whole with all the communal conveniences* (photo by ERIC DE MARÉ).

LEFT, *the Great Harbour Canal runs through the business centre of Gothenburg. On the left is the tower of the old German Church, also called Kristine kyrka, and, in front of it stands the East India Company building of the mid-eighteenth century, now housing among other things the Museum of Cultural History.*

BELOW, *a summer café outside Gothenburg's Town Theatre facing Götaplatsen. In the background is the Museum of Art* (photo by ERIC DE MARÉ).

ral for it is not a very large building; it was erected with a square tower and an austere neo-classical character in 1815 after a fire, the architect being C. W. Carlberg, son of B. W. Carlberg and nephew of J. E. Carlberg, Gothenburg's first municipal engineer and town planner.

MODERN HOUSING

Around the town to the east and south lie many new housing estates of flats and small dwellings. Perhaps among the best examples of housing on a planned, social scale is the Neighbourhood Unit of Guldheden which lies on the heights to the south and is soon reached by tram from the centre. Completed in 1950 for a private company, it is a good, typical example of modern, well-planned domesticity. The rocky, park-like site is laid out informally and the blocks of flats of brick or coloured stucco, some of them high Point Houses and some low Long Houses, most of them enjoying fine views, are set wide apart without stiff regimentation. All the conveniences are here. Around the market square, just off the main road, stand shops, a restaurant with a terrace, cinema, post office and a large *Kollektivhus*—the latter being a block of service flats designed especially for single people or married couples both of whom go to work each day and have therefore little time for domestic work.

The market square is a delightful area with a pond and informal garden close by bearing silver birches; the restaurant terrace is cheerful with flowers and coloured umbrellas. Another communal amenity here is an office where household help can be hired by the day or the hour and where mutual aid among tenants is organised, while up among the blocks of flats are other communal buildings—a laundry, a plant for heating the whole neighbourhood and fed by local rubbish, a garage and a nursery school. Below each block of flats is a communal drying room for home launderers and some of the blocks have large halls which can be hired for social occasions. As in all new Swedish flats rubbish chutes have been built into the walls with access openings at each landing.

Here at Guldheden life should be easy and enjoyable, for most of the practical domestic problems have been solved and many of the aesthetic and social problems too.

EXCURSIONS

From Gothenburg a number of summer resorts and fishing villages along the rocky coast can be reached, most of them by steamer. Among them is Särö, virtually an island lying about 15 miles south of the town, which is a summer suburb by the sea and a yachting centre with a hotel and restaurant. The most popular summer resort, however, is the island of Marstrand lying to the north and reached by steamer in about two hours. Marstrand is an island town with an ancient history; founded in the thirteenth century, it became an important centre for the herring fishing until the shoals moved elsewhere and brought local ruin. On the highest part of the island rises the ruined Carlsten Fort founded by the Danes but completed by the Swedes after 1658, from whose tower a magnificent view of the island and the neighbouring archipelago can be enjoyed. The view is particularly lovely on a summer evening when the rocks, black, austere and treeless, lie like prehistoric monsters dozing in the shining sea and the brilliant, lingering sunshine of the north lights up a distant white sail and sets ablaze the burning-red cottages of the fishermen.

An old print of the Göta River and Bohus Castle.

GOTHENBURG TO SJÖTORP

The canal steamers start from Lilla Bommen quay north of the town at about nine o'clock in the morning. Here is a time table of the 58-hour journey from Gothenburg to Stockholm as it is in 1964 when boats are running from 16 May until 9 September on three days of each week.

From Gothenburg to Stockholm

First Day

Gothenburg, Lilla Bommen	9.00 a.m.
Trollhättan (hotel)	15.30
Vänersborg (Lake Vänern)	16.30

Second Day

Sjötorp	1.00 a.m.
Töreboda	6.30
Rödesund (Lake Vättern)	11.15
Vadstena	15.00
Motala	16.00
Borensberg	18.30
Berg	22.30

Third Day

Norsholm	1.00 a.m.
Söderköping	6.00
Oxelösund (Baltic)	10.45
Södertälje	16.15
Arr. Stockholm, Riddarholmen	19.00

From Stockholm to Gothenburg

First Day

Stockholm, Riddarholmen	9.00 a.m.
Södertälje (lock)	11.30
Oxelösund	16.30
Söderköping	21.45

12

Second Day

Norsholm	3.15 a.m.
Berg (Brunnby)	6.45
Borensberg	9.45
Motala	12.30
Vadstena	15.00
Rödesund	16.45
Töreboda	22.00

Third Day

Sjötorp (Lake Vänern)	3.15 a.m.
Vänersborg	10.45
Trollhättan (hotel)	12.00
Trollhättan (locks)	13.30
Arr. Gothenburg, Lilla Bommen	18.00

Boats sailing from Stockholm on Fridays will call at Lidköping, which at no extra charge, increases the journey by four hours. When considering which way to travel do not forget that the northern twilight is very long in the summer, and in June at least full night never falls. When nights are fairly dark the steamers switch on their headlamps along the narrow reaches of the waterway, so adding to the enchantment of the northern night. Thus there is always something to be seen throughout each of the twenty-four hours should the voyager not be asleep in his berth.

BOHUS CASTLE AND KUNGÄLV

We steam up the Göta Älv, a wide river today though much narrower than it was when the ice cap was melting 10,000 years ago, for it was then a great fjord. The landscape is as yet unexciting; on the left lies Hisingen, the market garden of Gothenburg, on whose northern side flows the Nordre Älv, the subsidiary mouth of the Göta Älv.

In about half-an-hour from the start we shall see ahead a rocky escarpment on the top of which an old stone ruin stands silhouetted against the sky. It is Bohus Castle and it is distinguished by two round towers known as Father's Hat and Mother's Bonnet. Begun early in the fourteenth century this was one of the most important and strongest fortresses in Scandinavia, for, standing on an islet commanding the confluence of the Göta and Nordre Rivers, it served, at a vital strategic point, as a border fortress when Norway marched with Sweden along the river boundary. The castle grew apace in the 1440:ies, was strengthened and enlarged in the sixteenth century and reached its final form as a grand fortified palace in the first half of the seventeenth century under that great builder,

110

Bohus Castle, once the strongest fortress in Western Scandinavia (photo by ERIC DE MARÉ*).*

Bohus Castle and Kungälv, where the Nordre and the Göta Rivers join each

other. The Nordre River is to be seen to the right. The town is of medieval origin.

LEFT, *luncheon on board a Göta Canal passenger steamer.*

BELOW, *coffee is served on deck.*

"*An excellent déjeuner, for which purpose the little vessel has a small salle à manger, was truly welcome. The fare is good as need be, and extremely moderate in price; more perfect cleanliness and attention it is impossible to see, add to which, a silver fork, napkin, with fresh fish, eggs, and veritable cream, brought on board every morning, leave little to be desired in our floating cabaret.*"

ROBERT COLTON (SYLVANUS) in "*Rambles in Sweden and Gottland*" (1847).

Christian IV of Denmark. It remained a stronghold—one that was besieged fourteen times but never carried by assault—until 1658 when, with the Treaty of Roskilde, the place came into Swedish hands. After 1678, in the time of Carl XI, the castle lost most of its military importance. It was abandoned in the late eighteenth century, gradually fell into decay and was used as a quarry until in 1838 King Charles XIV (alias Bernadotte) happened to pass it on a river journey and forbade its further desecration. What is now left is preserved as a National Monument.

It was in 1308 during the later years of Norway's Great Age that King Håkon Magnusson began the building of Bohus as a military border base and a point of defence against the Swedes at a time when Bohuslän province belonged to Norway. It was later connected with many historical occasions—historical for Denmark as well as for Norway and Sweden, for in 1380 Denmark became united with Norway under one king. The castle became the seat of the Governors of Bohuslän right up to 1700.

The last attack the castle suffered in its bloody history was the worst—the attack of 1678 when Bohus was in Swedish hands. The Danes and Norwegians, 11,000 strong, were attempting to recapture it from some 900 Swedish defenders. After 49 days of siege no less than 2,265 bombshells, 600 large grenades, 161 red hot cannon balls and 79 baskets of hand grenades had been cast into the fortress—apart from thousands of ordinary cannon shots, petards and stones. Lethal stinkpots of human excrement were also hurled into the fortress by means of the catapults and, according to report, these produced "foul disease and burning fever" among the long-suffering defenders who were eventually relieved by a Swedish expeditionary force. By the end of the siege Christian IV's grand and decorated structure was in a sorry state and, though the building's defences were afterwards restored, it never regained its architectural nobility. Seeing it today a cynical visitor might say of it: "That was a ruin—once." Though still an imposing pile, none of its former glory now remains.

You can see how the castle looked in its prime in the year 1658 in an engraving by Erik Dahlbergh (1625-1703). Dahlbergh was himself a military engineer, a man of peasant stock who became a field-marshal. It was he who designed the two impressive forts of Gothenburg called Kronan and Lejonet which still stand. So expert at his job was he that both Charles II of England and Frederick III of Denmark asked for his services, but these he patriotically refused to give them. He was also a very accomplished architect as his church at Karlshamn reveals; his chief claim to fame, however, rests in the splendid book of copper engravings he made called "Suecia Antiqua et Hodierna" in which he has recorded for posterity both Sweden's ancient towns and buildings and the many grand new noblemen's palaces and gardens of his own expansive age.

Kungälv still exists as a charming riverside village which is worth visiting from Gothenburg, being only a 10-mile journey by bus or car. Apart from the castle, which is open to the public, the old wooden church of 1679 is interesting, not least on account of its interior objects—some curious ceiling paintings, some carved angels and a fine votive ship. Kungälv also has a tiny eighteenth-century town hall and an old inn where a first-class meal can be enjoyed by the waterside.

Kungälv is one of the oldest towns in Sweden and as far back as 1101 it was the conference centre of the three Scandinavian kings. In the early Middle Ages it became an important trading centre, one of Gothenburg's precursors. Originally called Kungahälla and guarded by the castle of Ragnhildsholmen, it has suffered much in its history from fire and pillage. In 1613 under Christian IV of Denmark the whole village was rebuilt on the island just below the protective walls of Bohus Castle. Again in 1679 the town was moved, or rather rebuilt on the opposite bank after the attack of 1676. Since that time the place has remained stable.

Beyond Bohus the hills come closer. The landscape assumes a more typically Swedish character with its rocks and pinewoods and soon we pass Lödöse on the right—only a quiet village today with a small dock, a few shops including a co-op and a pleasant church of 1845 with a square tower. Nothing now remains to show that in the Middle Ages Gamla Lödöse was an important, fortified market town and a port from where ships traded with England and Flanders. In time it came to own two churches, a monastery and a castle, but it suffered from the heavy tolls imposed by the hostile commanders of Bohus Castle on ships approaching it up the river and in the fourteenth and fifteenth centuries it was laid waste three times by invading Danes and Norwegians from across the river. In 1473, therefore, most af the inhabitants moved to a more comfortable spot nearer the river's mouth and there they founded Nya Lödöse which was the real precursor of Gothenburg.

After Lödöse the countryside becomes less inhabited; sometimes the river is wide with flat marshy banks and sometimes it narrows between rocks where it runs rapidly. Trees grow thickly on the banks and they are not always coniferous for oak trees are frequent. The Swedish character of landscape is never long absent, however, with its grey, lichen-clad granite, its fir trees below which the bilberries grow thickly and its occasional timber farmstead in its coat of brilliant winey red.

This red of the country farms and cottages is so typically and exclusively Swedish that something should be said now about this beautiful building colour. Most country buildings in Sweden are of sawn softwood and therefore they need protection. No better wood protection exists than this Swedish *Falu rödfärg* or red paint. But it has other qualities than that of

116

Ulrika Church and bell-tower in Östergötland, built in the eighteenth century, are typical timber structures protected by that rich Falu-red paint, which adds a special charm to the Swedish landscape (photo by JAN MARK).

preservation: cheapness and beauty of colour—a rich, warm, ruddy purple with a matt texture. It harmonizes perfectly with the landscape, acting as a complement to the surrounding grey of the rocks and dark green of the fir trees and creating vivid spots of colour to enliven a scene which, for all its typical charm, might otherwise grow monotonous. But Falu Red never grows boring as a colour, perhaps because its shades vary subtly from place to place and from time to time. Reflecting the evening sunlight on the rocky west coast it is fantastic in its brilliance, while among the whites and greys of winter in the countryside it is more quietly gay.

Falu Red, this red ochre of Sweden, is a natural, indigenous material. Its main source of supply is the copper mine of Falun in Dalarna, which is owned by the oldest trading company in the world—the Stora Koppar-bergs Bergslags Aktiebolag, founded in the thirteenth century and still flourishing as one of the largest industrial concerns in the country. A by-product of its copper mine is the *rödfärgsmull* or Red Earth, composed partly of iron oxides from which the paint is made.

The mining of *rödfärgsmull* did not begin until the latter half of the eighteenth century and was used at first only on important buildings such as churches and manor houses, but later it came into general use for farms as production rose and as timber became more expensive and required greater protection. Falu Rödfärg is still used extensively in Sweden today. If it were ever to be replaced by duller materials, some virtue which is more than physical would leave the land.

A SMALL TOWN

The next place of interest on the Göta River is Lilla Edet and here the steamer climbs the first lock which is worked by electricity from the power station close by. Lilla Edet is just a small market town with a factory or two, including a paper mill. Most small towns like this in Sweden have ancient origins but they rarely possess many old buildings on account of the fires which have repeatedly ravaged their timber structures in the past. Lilla Edet, for instance, was last burned down in 1888. Today fire regulations, piped water, efficient fire-fighting services and fire-proof construction have almost eliminated the old fire risk but much of ancient Sweden unhappily disappeared in smoke and flames before these aids arrived.

The relics of the urban past which remain today reveal that the old country town was largely composed of clusters of wooden buildings sur-rounding private courtyards, somewhat like the farmsteads of the open countryside. The old country village communities were not only broken up by fire in the past, however; the Storskifte of the 1750:ies, a kind of Enclosures Act procedure, did not greatly affect the old communities, but

117

the Enskifte Act of 1803-4 did so drastically, for then parcels of land were exchanged in order that united farms could be created; the result was that many peasants moved out to the country away from the villages to new homes set in the midst of their new land. Today the tendency of country people to congregate in compact villages is returning.

TROLLHÄTTAN

We pass other villages and five hours after leaving Gothenburg we enter the dramatic, rocky defile below the Trollhätte locks. Here at the first lock passengers can land for about two hours to explore the neighbourhood while the steamer works its way up the 105 feet of the giant flight of modern locks—locks which can pass ships carrying over 2,100 tons.

Trollhättan is a modern industrial and marketing centre of some 33,000 inhabitants depending to a certain extent on the cheap power obtainable from the hydro-electric station here. The two main features of visual interest in the town are the great market place and the pleasant waterside parks which are laid out on the long islands of the river, many of which were formed when the power station was built.

The two hours here are probably best spent in exploring, not the town itself, but the area between the passage of the old falls and the modern canal. Here can be seen the disused locks of 1800 and 1844 and one of Polhem's abortive locks of the mid-eighteenth century; also, among many other things, a curious ice-age grotto or glacial cauldron, seven feet wide, where royal visitors have carved their names since the eighteenth century. Although only on special occasions is the water of the once famous Trollhätte Falls now allowed to drop down 106 feet on its original course in six great torrents, the glen itself is still impressive. The two great State-owned power stations are also worth a visit.

The first of these, Olide Station, was built in 1910-19, the largest in the country at the time, and the other one, Hojum Station, was built between 1927 and 1942. These hydro-electric works are the most important in southern Sweden and through their turbines most of the water of the old falls is now directed in order to produce a maximum capacity of 240,000 kilowatts. Enough water passes through the power-houses here every second, it is said, to supply the daily needs of 3,200 townspeople. The stations are linked up with others in the country on a national grid and, so long as a summer is not too dry, this White Coal of Sweden's waterfalls provides a rich source of power some of which is even exported to Denmark.

118

ABOVE, *occasionally the waterfall of Trollhättan ceases to turn the turbines and is re-directed in its old channel—a spectacle which always attracts a large crowd.*

RIGHT, *a canal bridge at Trollhättan.*

"*The Canal reminded me of our Irish project to cut Ireland also right across from Galway to Dublin, only a hundred miles, thus making a direct waterway for the American steamers from the Atlantic to the Irish Sea. But the Swedes accomplished their project, while we only talked of ours, though no difficulty was involved in the construction.*"

JANE FRANCESCA WILDE *in* "*Driftwood from Scandinavia*" *(1884).*

ABOVE, *the Trollhättan waterfall released into its natural course.*

LEFT, *the curious stone carving by Carl Eldh of the head of* "*Strömkarlen*" *(God of the Waters) serves as a decorative bridge pier at the hydro-electric power station of Trollhättan.*

"*Should an age of darkness again envelop Scandinavia, and bring back the reign of ignorance and super-stition, the works of Trollhättan, like those of the Romans, would doubtless be ascribed to giants, fairies or gods*"

JOSEPH ACERBI *in "Travels through Sweden" (1802).*

RIGHT, *one of the locks of 1916 at Trollhättan which can accomodate ships of nearly 15 feet draught.*

OVERLEAF, "*From the Baltic coast a canal reaching right across Sweden takes you to the first of the Great Lakes. The canal follows a depres-sion which forms a natural way from sea to lake, though not without a 'saddle' which has to be crossed by locks. That depression was followed by commerce for centuries, and a great tower built by the Wasas dominates over the narrows.*
These immense inland waters, almost seas, would be of prodigious effect in any of the more populated parts of Europe. Imagine a sheet of navig-able water 100 miles by 40 in the midst of England or France. What history would have gathered round it, what shrines, what great cities."

HILAIRE BELLOC *in "Return to the Baltic" (1938).*

ABOVE, *Lake Vänern in a wild mood. The lake is Sweden's largest at 2,123 square miles. The Göta River provides it with an outlet to the sea.*

RIGHT, *Lake Vänern seen from Halleberg, one of the many hills of Västergötland, having precipitous sides and flat tops.*

ABOVE, *the baroque castle of Läckö seen from the air.*

LEFT, *the approach to the inner courtyard of the castle (photo by* ERIC DE MARÉ).

HUNNEBERG AND HALLEBERG

We re-embark at the quay by the Town Hall above the locks and passing under a railway structure, which is the largest swing bridge in Scandinavia, we steam along an attractive reach called the Stallbacka Canal. Soon two strange hills with precipitous sides and flat tops appear on the right. These are called Hunneberg (505 feet high) and Halleberg (509 feet high); they are typical of a local type of rock formation. Within the woods around these hills more elk roam wild than in any other part of the world and they are hunted still during a very short open season. The author has himself explored Halleberg, the more northern of the two hills, and he found it a weird, lonely, haunted place, quite unlike the cultivated and inhabited countryside around. Here, in fact, is one of the few remaining royal forests in southern Sweden, a place rich in legend and in ancient remains which include signs of pre-historic man and a number of Viking burial mounds.

KARLS GRAV

At Brinkebergskulle we turn left off the river and enter the old Karls Grav, or Charles's Cut, the oldest part of the Trollhätte Canal, which was begun early in the seventeenth century in the time of Charles IX, a son of Gustavus Vasa. Its purpose is to provide a way through to Lake Vänern so that the Rännum Falls, the first on the Göta River, can be by-passed. Today those falls are used, like those at Trollhätte, to make electricity.

Behind us in the distance at the base of Hunneberg we can see a white building. It is Nygård where Nils Ericson, the canal and railway engineer and brother of John Ericson, lived for some time; he lies buried in West Tunhem Church which stands about a mile and a half to the south of Nygård.

We mount a lock and proceed for two miles until we reach the small lake of Vassbotten to the north of which appears the pleasant old town of Vänersborg standing on a promontory of Lake Vänern between round and reedy Lake Vassbotten and the Göta River. We navigate the sound between Vassbotten and Vänern through a remarkable railway bridge which has the largest single bascule in Europe, 130 feet high when raised. Beyond this the steamer moors for a short while, but not for long enough to allow passengers to go ashore.

VÄNERSBORG

Vänersborg, a town of about 19,000 inhabitants, is the capital of the administrative county or *län* of Älvsborg. It was founded in Queen Christina's time in the middle of the seventeenth century but like so many towns in Sweden it has been burned and harried by invaders several times. In 1834 a terrible fire destroyed the whole place except for the church and the imposing Governor's Residence, both of which were built in the eighteenth century and still survive. Besides these two buildings, Vänersborg is notable for its delightful lakeside park laid out with that subtle sensitivity to landscaping which is a Swedish virtue. This park has another advantage than being a beautiful recreation area; its trees protect the town from the great north winds which sweep down the 87 open miles of the great lake.

The opening of the canal in the early nineteenth century brought a new prosperity to Vänersborg but it still retains its quiet provincialism.

LAKE VÄNERN

For the next eight hours—from about half-past five in the afternoon until one o'clock in the morning—we shall be steaming across Lake Vänern through the brilliant evening and the long, lingering twilight of the North. This lake is the largest in Sweden and the third largest in all Europe (following Ladoga and Onega), being 2,123 square miles in area. Like Vättern to its east, Vänern is a sheet of water left behind by the sea as it receded after the Ice Age, and that it was once a huge inlet of the sea the grey salmon still swimming in its waters bear witness.

Lying 144 feet above sea level it has a depth of 302 feet at its northern end. It is fed by several rivers and is drained by only one—the Göta Älv; thus it serves as a splendid natural reservoir for the three power stations on that river, as well as a useful navigation and a general water supply. Its water is cool and clean and, except near the towns, the local inhabitants around its shores take their drinking water directly from it. The southern part of the lake is divided into two parts by the Värmlandsnäs peninsula at the north of which lies the island of Kållandsö. The steamer will skirt round this island and its rocky archipelago and in the distance on the north-east of the island we may be able to glimpse the square white walls and towers of the famous Castle of Läckö. Unfortunately no means has yet been found of organizing a stop here for the passenger steamers; a brief description of this interesting place may be welcome here all the same.

LÄCKÖ CASTLE

In the Middle Ages it belonged to the bishops of Skara but it was taken over by Gustavus Vasa at the Reformation. In 1615 King Gustavus Adolphus gave it to Jacob De la Gardie, a nobleman, who married the King's sweetheart Ebba Brahe. Some years later their son, Count Magnus Gabriel De

128

The motorship Juno in a lock on the Göta Canal.

la Gardie (1622—86), Chancellor, favourite of Queen Christina and an enthusiastic builder, converted it into the bold baroque palace we now see, a mansion so large that it is surpassed in size in Sweden only by the Royal Palace in Stockholm.

Charles XI confiscated it in 1681 at the time when he was reducing the power and extravagance of the nobility. In 1830 all the interior furnishings, even the painted panels, were auctioned by the Crown at knock-down prices; fine gobelin tapestries, for instance, went to local peasants for a few shillings and were used for carpets or horse blankets. Today the State looks after the place as a museum and much of the original furniture and decorations have now been reinstated. Therefore we can here gain a vivid impression of how a seventeenth-century Swedish nobleman's palace really looked.

The sturdy pile contains 248 rooms grouped round two spacious courtyards—an inner and an outer—as well as a narrow kitchen yard to the north. Off the kitchen yard is a curiosity of the place—a well sunk through the rock to a depth of 90 feet and connected to the lake half-way down by a tunnel which provided, not only an inlet to the water, but also a last way of escape in case of siege. It is called the Pork Well (Fläskgraven) because in its engineering the rock was broken away by the burning of no less than 300 fat hams. The rock was heated with a burning ham and was then suddenly allowed to cool so that it cracked; with the help of iron levers, the large pieces of split rock could be removed. The old pump of the well made in 1678 is also curious, being operated by a man's swinging on a huge oak beam.

The state rooms are on the upper floors, the finest of them being the banqueting hall, called Riddarsalen or Hall of the Knights, which is decorated with ceiling panels painted with groups of arms and flying cherubim by a foreign artist, Johan Werner; between the deep window reveals are further painted panels in the form of large battle scenes of the Thirty Years' War executed by various painters of the time. At the north end of the hall is a carved screen with a servery and a gallery above it where musicians could play unseen and remain blind themselves to the roistering below.

The best interior in the palace is the light and airy chapel where Christina once worshipped. Its window reveals are adorned with a fine set of saints' figures carved in wood and painted, some by Johan Werner, who was an accomplished sculptor as well as a painter, others by another foreigner—Georg Baselaque.

KINNEKULLE

Beyond the peninsular to the east we can see the great isolated hill of Kinnekulle, which, rising nearly 900 feet above the lake, dominates the

129

landscape across the bay called Viken. At the south end of this bay lies the town of Lidköping; founded by Magnus Gabriel De la Gardie it is now an industrial centre containing, among other works, the Rörstrand Potteries and the largest town square in Sweden.

Kinnekulle with its surrounding district is a famous beauty spot, rich in colourful vegetation and wild life, a place where Carl von Linné, the naturalist, loved to roam. The strange hill, like Halleberg and Hunneberg, consists of soft rock surmounted and protected by a layer of hard volcanic diabase —the result of some prehistoric upheaval. The name was formerly Kindakulle, *kulle* meaning hill and *kinda* or *kinna* meaning to kindle a fire; it is therefore Beacon Hill. Many strange, stratified rock formations and grottos are found among the fertile woods and here and there stand old and interesting buildings, notably the ancient church of Husaby, the centre of the first see in Sweden from which Christianity spread throughout Västergötland. It was at this place in 1008 that Olof Skötkonung may have been baptized to become the first Christian king of the country.

SJÖTORP

Beyond the Djurö lighthouse we turn east and pass several large islands lying to the north of Mariestad, the homely county town of Skaraborg. In the small, quiet, twilit hours we glide by the twinkling light of a little white timber lighthouse and arrive at the lake-side port of Sjötorp where the Western Line of the Göta Canal proper begins—the early-nineteenth-century cut of Platen and Telford. Here is a quay, the first of the canal superintendent's offices, a dry dock, a sweet-smelling timber yard and a village community. From here to Mem on the Baltic all the locks are of the old-fashioned sort, only 98 feet long and with their beams and sluices all worked by human muscles.

When it was first built the canal must have been a depressing sight with muddy banks and every sign of a violent human attack on nature. But nature soon reclaims her own so that today the old canal seems to be a natural part of the landscape and looks more like a smiling river than a man-made cut, with its quiet water lovingly enfolded by grassy, tree-lined banks. At the time the canal was being built, tow-paths were constructed along both banks where horses or oxen could haul the boats and then miles of hardwood trees were planted along them—trees which are now reaching

RIGHT, *The great lakes of Sweden, like Vänern and Vättern, provide splendid waters for amateur yachtsmen.*

130

Wild water lilies grow profusely in the backwaters of the countryside.

A skiff on Lake Vänern displays its Viking ancestry (photo by ERIC DE MARÉ*).*

LEFT, *a little lighthouse of timber on the shores of Lake Vänern.*

BELOW, *an old trading schooner enters a lock at Sjötorp (photos by* ERIC DE MARÉ).

their maturity. Though these tow-paths are not used today for their original purpose and in parts are overgrown, they were so used until quite recent time. Today they form green and bosky tracks for cyclists and country walkers and add to the scenic pleasure of a canal journey.

An old wood engraving of Sjötorp harbour.

SJÖTORP TO VADSTENA

At Sjötorp the steamer begins to mount a series of eight locks extending for a mile or so through wooded country. Another 10 locks will be climbed before the summit level is reached at Lake Viken. During the early hours we shall no doubt be sleeping below but not a great deal will be missed of interest and the scenery here is not exceptional, being somewhat flat and marshy. The first village to be passed is Lyrestad, a small centre with a canal basin and old timber warehouses in Falu Red which von Platen had hoped to develop as one of his large new canal towns; in that he was disappointed and in the end the only one of his new towns along the waterway which has grown to any size has been Motala.

A legend is still current about these parts: When Platen sent his representative to arrange the purchase of lands for the building of the canal he was faced with considerable opposition from the local peasant owners. An astute man, the agent then started a whispering campaign: "You see where the canal is going to run? Well, have you ever seen water flowing up hill? The canal will never be built. Sell your land now and when the project fails you will be able to buy it back again at a much lower price than that for which you sold it." The story relates that this ruse worked well, the peasants sold their land without further hesitation but they never regained it.

Of course, when a large project like the Göta Canal is built an Enabling Act must be passed by the government to permit the acquisition of the necessary land. This always leads to resentments, difficulties, arguments and legal complications. Eventually the Göta Canal Company was forced to pay far more for the land it needed than had been estimated. Where direct financial compensation was not paid, owners received state-owned land in exchange for that which they had forfeited and, where possible, land was reparcelled so that whole properties could be formed on one side of the

FACING PAGE TOP, *an oil tanker enters a lock at Hajstorp*. BELOW, *midsummer night at Tåtorp on the Göta Canal (photos by* ERIC DE MARÉ).

136

canal only. Where that was not possible the Company was compelled to provide owners with accomodation bridges.

THE SUMMIT LEVEL

At about 6.30 in the morning we pass Töreboda, a place of interest only as a point where the Gothenburg—Stockholm railway crosses the canal. Soon we reach the watershed and the summit level at Lanthöjden. Here the canal is only 24 feet wide in some parts, having been blasted through solid rock. From this point as far as Lake Vättern the canal landscape is at its most wild, remote and beautiful, especially now in the genial morning light as the sun tops the trees.

A new cut at the summit point was made between 1930 and 1933 as part of the emergency public works programme of the World Slump period, the object being to cut off an unnecessary bend; we shall therefore not be able to see the large obelisk, hewn from granite, which was erected on the bank of the original cut to mark the highest point of the waterway.

At the hamlet of Tåtorp we enter the regulating lock between the canal and Lake Viken and, while the ship is locking through, a few minutes will be available to send off a card at the village post office here. We now enter charming Lake Viken, 15 miles long, narrow, twisting, encircled with forest and dappled with islands. It was in this lake that Platen had such trouble in 1824. We round the high land of Vika Forest on the right while on the left we pass Halna Church and then the mouth of Sätraån. This river runs down from Lake Unden, an auxiliary source of water to Lake Viken which in its turn supplies the Västgöta Line of the canal with its water. A short distance up the river lies the hamlet of Sätra where Telford and Platen centered their work when they were laying out the line of the canal.

Through a narrow stretch called Brosundet, past the islet of Kidön and then a turn right into a short cut of the Edet Canal where you can almost pluck the leaves from the overhanging trees as the little white steamer hisses gently past them. Then across the tail of Viken, through the short Bilström

LEFT, *summer evening on the Västgöta Line between Sjötorp and Forsvik, near the Summit Level. "The marvellous canal wound up the mountains—higher and higher, through woods exquisite as Westermain of the Legends, widening into lovely bays and lakelets, with chalets from Hans Chr. Andersen in every nook. It seemed so unreal to be gliding between pine carpets, and to have birch boughs brushing our mast so high in the hills, and then to have to halt to let a great timber barque pass us, in such mountain fields, rich with barley and potatoes, and with the smell of wood fires all about"* (FRANCES G. KNOWLES-FOSTER *in* The Daily Express 6/4 1926).

which joins Viken with Lake Botten and we are in the Forsvik millpond with its sawmill and its floating logs.

FORSVIK

Forsvik is a very old, small industrial centre which belonged to Vadstena Monastery way back in the fifteenth century. Then a sawmill was constructed here, the oldest one known to have existed in Sweden. The community now depends almost entirely on a large timber works and the place is a typical example of the decentralised industries of Sweden which can often be found isolated in the middle of the country. Forsviks Skogar (Forests) is the name of the concern here which owns the local sawmill and much of the forest land around.

It is said that if the canal between Vättern and Vänern were widened to the size of the Trollhätte Canal so that it could carry sea-going ships, this enterprise could save some £ 8,000 a year in transport costs because trans-shipping at Gothenburg would then be unnecessary for export goods. Other factories such as paper and wood-pulp mills situated around Lake Vättern, which now mostly use the railways, would also benefit greatly by this improvement of communication.

At Forsvik we enter the first lock on our downward journey—a very deep one and the first lock built on the canal (1813). The little iron bascule bridge above the lock is interesting for it was made in England at the time the canal was building. It has been nicely described by a Swedish writer as being "as English as an iron bedstead". Sadly enough, it is doomed and is replaced by a more modern, but a less endearing, structure. Anyhow, the old bridge is left on the site as a monument.

THE ERICSON BROTHERS

Forsvik was an important centre during the construction of the canal and it was here that the brothers John and Nils Ericson, who were to become such famous engineers, were brought from Värmland by their parents when they were only seven and eight years old. Their father had given up his job in a foundry to engage in the canal works and to superintend the blasting operations on the Västgöta Line. The sons became apprentices on the canal and eventually employees. John was soon considered competent enough to be placed in charge of 600 men though still only a boy of 14 and so small that he was compelled to stand on a stool when using his surveying instrument. As already related, he went to America and settled there to become a Jules Verne character in the real world. On his death his body was sent back to Sweden to be buried at Filipstad in his home county of Värmland. Nils was engaged in different work on the canal, including masonry, and at the age of 22 became foreman for the Östgöta Line. On the left bank, just before the bridge, you can see a pleasant timber house painted in Falu Red. There the Ericson family lived and there Mrs. E. ran a canteen for the canal's local executive staff during the building of the waterway.

KARLSBORG

Beyond Forsvik we enter Lake Botten or Bottensjön, and at high noon we tie up at the quay of the canal station of Rödesund which lies on the strait between the little Botten and mighty Vättern. Ahead of us is a promontory called Vanäs on which stands the military fortress and barracks of Karlsborg. Founded in 1820 in the time of Charles XIV and completed in 1845, its purpose was to serve as a central base forming part of Platen's strategic scheme of national defence, of which the canal itself was an essential element; in fact, during the construction of the canal Platen had planned a large dockyard at Söderköping as a centre for the archipelago fleet. The fortress is a remarkable pile, rude and vigorous, of earthworks, heavy stone fortifications, squat round corner towers and barrack buildings which must form the longest coherent edifice in Europe.

LAKE VÄTTERN

We shall now steam across the north of Lake Vättern enjoying the great, refreshing space of sky and water until in about an hour-and-a-half we reach Vadstena and Östergötland. Vättern is a strange lake, nearly 80 miles from north to south and only 19 miles wide at its widest. The fourth largest lake in Europe, it lies 290 feet above the sea and is no less than 420 feet deep at its deepest places—so deep indeed that the water near the bottom remains near freezing point all the year round. Its water is so clear that sometimes the bottom in some areas is visible to a depth of 50 feet. It is really a great fissure—a huge cleft—in Sweden's central ridge and, though it is fed by a number of small streams, its main source of water is believed to be subterranean, thus making it a vast spring. Its only outlet is the Motala Ström to the east which drains it to the Baltic.

The lake has always been regarded with a certain awe on account of its moody and unpredictable nature and its mysterious habits. Old folk tales tell of its terrors and its magic. At one moment it is serene and loving, then suddenly the sky darkens and within a few minutes it is a lashing shrew. But its strangest habit is its burping—its periodic cannonading which is particularly audible in the quiet days of early spring and is believed to be caused by gases which rise to the surface as the bedrock settles.

Vättern's water is of light weight and this, no doubt, is one reason for its sudden and unpredictable storms and its choppy seas which come in spasms of three waves at a time—a feature which the local yachtsmen know well for they are always ready for the third wave to splash aboard. On calm days a slight breeze will send lines of ripples across its surface which appear like straight and defined roads; these are called the Roads of St. Bridget (Birgitta) who, according to legend, would often walk to church across Lake Boren—that lake not far to the east into which Vättern's water flows.

Visingsö, the only large island on the lake, lies to the south but it is too far off to be visible. Far to the south of the lake lies the match town of Jönköping, while to the south-east we can see Mount Omberg rising; it was an island surrounded by cold seas at the time the ice cap was melting.

An old vignette of Vadstena Castle.

RIGHT, *Lake Vättern from Omberg.* "*. . . so clear and blue that when smooth it looks like a mirror of blue glass. But the mariner at times dreads its surface, which is very sensitive, and without warning is often stirred up without any apparent cause. It is also noted for its eddies, whirlpools and mirages*" (PAUL DU CHAILLU *in "The Land of the Midnight Sun," 1881).*

142

ABOVE, *the approach to Vadstena Castle.* BELOW, *the breakwater at Vadstena and, in the distance, the church of St. Bridget's monastery (photos by* ERIC DE MARÉ*).*

VADSTENA

The approach to Vadstena by water is monumental. On the left a small white timber lighthouse at the end of a long breakwater stands guard at the entrance to the short approach canal. The breakwater runs into a wooded strip of parkland and across it on the far side of a bay rise the roof and the elegant flêche of the Vadstena monastery church, while in the foreground below the trees along the waterfront runs a row of sleek yachts and other craft including, maybe, an old timber schooner. Right ahead the grand stone pile of Vadstena Castle, dominating the pleasing prospect with its low round bastions and soaring baroque spires, stands firmly in the midst of its encircling moat. We shall moor below the castle for about two hours and in that time we can explore some parts of this old and attractive little town—one of the richest in the country in historical and cultural associations and the central climax of our cross-country voyage.

Vadstena has only about 4,600 inhabitants yet some 40,000 tourists visit the place every year. It is not merely a show place, however, for it remains a lake-side shipping centre and it has several factories, schools and hospital institutions, besides a market and many shops. And it is still famed for the traditional local handicraft of lace-making which has been carried on here for at least two centuries.

In the year 1400 Queen Margaret of Denmark and Sweden granted the town its municipal charter and privileges and for centuries thereafter Vadstena held an important position in the religious, political and cultural life not only of Östergötland but of all Sweden. St. Bridget was the cause of that.

St. Bridget—Birgitta Birgersdotter, (1303-1373)—one of the most remarkable and energetic women in Swedish history, founded a monastic Order which was to turn a little lake-side settlement into the most important religious centre in the North and from there to spread throughout Europe.

Bridget was born on an Uppland farm, the daughter of the governor and county judge of Uppland, Birger Persson, and his wife, Ingeborg Bengtsdotter, who was related to the powerful Folkunga family. In 1316 at the age

145

of 14 she married a young man of 18 called Ulf Gudmarsson and settled down at Ulvåsa farm on the southern shore of Lake Boren, a spot we shall pass when we continue our journey. There she lived for 20 years and there she bore eight children. In 1335 she was residing at the court of her relative King Magnus Eriksson and his young French queen and four years later she set out on a number of pilgrimages with her husband, visiting Nidaros in Norway, now called Trondheim, and various religious centres on the Continent. On one of these journeys her husband fell ill, the family returned to Sweden and in 1344 at the monastery of Alvastra on the east coast of Vättern he died.

Bridget was a visionary and after her husband's death her psychic revelations increased. All these she set down in her"Revelationes," and in one of her trances she claimed that Christ had revealed to her the rules of a new monastic Order which she was to found. In 1349, therefore, she set off for Rome with her daughter Catherine and others. There she remained for most of the 24 years she yet had to live and she never again saw her native land. Much of her energy in Rome was devoted to obtaining the Pope's sanction for her proposed new Order of St. Saviour and in 1370 her desire was at last fulfilled when her Order was authorised by Pope Urban V. Its rules were unusual and included the stipulation that the monasteries of the Order would contain both monks and nuns sharing a common church. In 1372 Bridget began a long pilgrimage to Jerusalem accompanied by three of her children. Having lost a son on her journey she returned wearily to Rome and there died in 1373. Her remains were sent back to Sweden and interred in the monastery church she had founded. Some 20 years later she was canonized by Pope Boniface IX.

Bridget had been permitted to found only one joint monastery and this she planned herself, an unusual feature being the placing of the monks' choir at the west end of the church. Bridget may thus be said to have been the first woman architect of the North. It was left to her daughter Catherine to complete the building of Vadstena monastery and church, for their building had only begun when Bridget died and they were not consecrated until 1430, 57 years after her death. The Order then spread rapidly until there were 80 Bridgetine houses in Europe. In England one survives still at South Brent in Devonshire. It is called Syon Abbey.

RIGHT, *St. Bridget (Birgitta), a wood carving of the fifteenth century in Vadstena Monastery Church.*

Vadstena Castle, founded by Gustav Vasa in the sixteenth century, is the finest Renaissance

building which Sweden has to offer. In the distance spreads the fertile plain of Östergötland.

ABOVE, *the entrance to Vadstena Castle across its encircling moat (photo by* ERIC DE MARÉ).

LEFT, *one of the bastions and the moat (photo by* ERIC DE MARÉ).

VADSTENA CASTLE

So much for the background. Let us now step ashore and take the town, first looking at Vadstena Castle close by. It is a grand and simple stone fortress consisting of a main block with a central tower, a spacious court-yard behind which was originally surrounded on three sides by massive walls and ramparts (lightened in 1850), and four squat round bastions at each corner, the whole being protected by a wide moat fed from Lake Vättern.

Vadstena was a strong Catholic centre and it is easy to understand why Gustavus Vasa, who brought the Reformation to Sweden, should have decided to build a stronghold here. He began building in 1545, using stones and other materials from the disestablished monasteries at Skänninge and Alvastra. The place was later much enlarged and decorated by his second son, John III, in the 1570:ies. After that Swedish royalty held court here right up to the death in 1715 of Hedvig Eleonora, Charles X's wife. Then it fell into decay, became a granary and for a while housed the Flemish linen weavers who brought the art of lace-making to the town. Today the interior is bare and much of it is used for the storing of national archives.

Vadstena Castle is the most developed of the several Vasa castles; its character is distinctly Renaissance and classical in that crude early way we would call Jacobean. It has axial symmetry, for example, whereas Grips-holm Castle (1537; see page 220) is still asymmetrical and retains several Gothic features. In all these castles the defensive moat remains from the past but, with the development of artillery, the old high keep with castella-tions and projections was replaced by low, circular bastions where cannon could be placed to face in all directions. These castles were at one and the same time fortresses, garrison depots and royal residences, and in their latter capacity received lavish decorations, mainly from foreign craftsmen, since sufficient skill was not available at that time within the country. At Vadstena Castle, for instance, the fine decorated gables with their niches and allegorical figures accomplished in 1605 and 1620 are the work of the Fle-mish architect and sculptor Hans Fleming and the German Bernt von Müns-ter, while the splendid main entrance in Italian style is by the Dutch sculp-tor Pierre de la Roche. The double lantern and ogee roof of the central tower and the smaller side turrets at the rear are baroque and were added by the architect Jean de la Vallée in 1657. The old drawbridge has gone for it was replaced by the present stone bridge in 1827. In spite of the various contributions which have been made at different times, the castle retains a remarkable and a monumental homogeneity.

Inside the castle there still remain some things of interest to see in those parts which are open to the public, but steamer passengers, who have only a short time to spend at Vadstena, are advised to concentrate their attention in and around the monastery church. For their information, however, the following points can be mentioned: the Chapel Hall (Kyrksalen) on the third floor has a magnificent Gothic star-vault of brickwork and two fine rose windows. On the second floor is Bröllopssalen (the Wedding Hall) in which Gustavus Vasa was married in his old age to the sixteen-year-old Catherine Stenbock. In the lowest landing of the south-west staircase tower is an opening in the wall which is a curiosity for it reveals a speaking tube by means of which warning of enemy approach could be given to the guard below from a small tower-room on the third floor.

VADSTENA CHURCH AND MONASTERY

Let us now stroll through the lake-side park to the Monastery Church founded by St. Bridget. Outside it is plain but impressive with broad buttresses, a bold roof and a tall flêche rising above it. We enter the building by a door at the east end of the south aisle and come into a very simple, spacious fane built of a blue-grey limestone from Omberg. The colour of the stone may have given the building its familiar name of the Blue Church. According to St. Bridget's precepts all the ways of her Order were to be unaffected and its buildings "of plain workmanship, humble and strong" and that character has here been achieved as an impressive piece of medieval functionalism. The eight sturdy octagonal piers support an unusual kind of vaulting, a sort of simplified star vaulting with narrow ribs of exposed brickwork rising to 100 feet above the floor, ribs which merge with hardly any articulation into the columns to create an effect of palm trees. The aisles are as wide and as high as the nave and this adds to the arboreal impression. At Vadstena, though the influence was Cistercian, a distinct Gothic style was established—the Bridgetine or Birgitta Style—bold and unornamented but impressive in its calm, spacious and dignified simplicity. The whole building was well restored about 1890; the stained-glass windows were added at that time but otherwise the church has not been seriously degraded.

Though the building itself is undecorated, many free-standing objects of beauty and interest decorate the interior. Proceeding round the church clockwise we shall especially note the following:—

(i) The triptych altar-piece on the south wall begun by Hans Hesse of Lübeck, completed by John Stenradh and erected in the church in 1459; in its centre panel St. Bridget is seen presenting books of her Revelations to a group of kneeling cardinals.

(ii) The distinguished Madonna and Child against the south-west wall carved in wood about 1500 possibly by a north-German artist.

152

ABOVE, *the interior of Vadstena Monastery Church in the simple Cistercian style.* RIGHT, *the Madonna and Child, a woodcarving of about 1500, is perhaps the most beautiful object in the church (photos by* ERIC DE MARÉ).

ABOVE, *parts of Vadstena monastery itself have survived, including this vaulted room of the fifteenth century.* BELOW, *the hospital of Mårten the Furrier at Vadstena dates from about 1520.*

(iii) The baptismal font on the axis of the nave near the west end ascribed to Pierre de la Roche, who is believed to have worked on the main entrance of the Castle in the middle of the sixteenth century.

(iv) The rood cross hanging from the rood arch at the west end of the nave—another north-German work, possibly of the mid-fifteenth century, ascribed to Johannes Junge of Lübeck.

(v) A triptych altar-piece below the cross, well preserved, by the renowned Jan Borman of Brussels which was a gift to the monastery from its chief confessor in 1521; the right panel depicts St. Ursula of whom the story is told that she was assassinated with 11,000 virgins at Cologne—an unusual and surprising event.

(vi) The reliquary to the left of it, said to contain the remains of St. Bridget and her daughter Catherine.

(vii) Some fine Flemish vestments of the end of the fifteenth century at the west end of the choir.

(viii) Five large confessional niches on the north wall of the choir where the monks once heard the confessions of the nuns who remained cloistered in their nunnery on the other side of the wall—a silent comment on the peculiar sex-life of the Middle Ages.

(ix) Two wooden statues of St. Bridget standing against the second pair of pillars from the east—the one to the north being possibly by Johannes Junge of Lübeck and the other a work done in the monastery.

(x) An exceptional carving of the figure of St. Jerome made at the end of the fifteenth century standing against the pillar furthest to the south-east which may have been the work of Henning von der Heide, an apprentice of that master Bernt Notke of Lübeck who made the famous St. George and the Dragon group standing in Stockholm's Storkyrka (Great Church; see page 204).

(xi) The ornamented baroque pews of the end of the seventeenth century standing just inside the south-east entrance on both sides of the door.

There are other things of interest in the church, notably some tombs and monuments of famous people. One had to be both famous and wealthy to be buried at Vadstena for it was an honour and cost a great deal of land in the old days. Among the sepulchres is the grand sarcophagus of sandstone and marble with recumbent figure on top which stands in the nave towards the south-east and is ascribed to Hans Fleming and Bernt von Münster; it was erected to Duke Magnus of Östergötland, the third son of Gustavus Vasa, an unstable character who died in 1595; one of his more peculiar acts which have been recorded was to throw himself from one of the windows of Vadstena Castle, apparently without coming to any harm, in order "to embrace a lovely female form which arose from the lake" (The sex-life of the Reformation period also had its odd expressions).

155

Other tombs are those of Bo Jonsson Grip, a grand lord of the Middle Ages; of Birger and Cecilia, two of Bridget's children; of Queen Philippa, daughter of Henry IV of England, wife of Eric, King of Sweden, Denmark and Norway and Duke of Pomerania, who died in 1430 and was a protectress of Vadstena Monastery.

Parts of the original nunnery to the north of the church remain and are reached across a leafy courtyard. Most of the place was until recently occupied by the Vadstena Mental Asylum for Women, but this hospital has been moved to another place, and the nunnery has been restored. Among other rooms two vaulted halls of the nunnery can be visited—the Chaper House and the Refectory. The decorative baroque doorway by which the halls are entered has a tympanum carved with military emblems dating from 1687, a year in the reign of Charles XI when the nunnery was a home for invalid soldiers from the Thirty Years' War. In an arched corridor here can be seen a genuine Bridgetine nun's dress as worn long ago at Syon Abbey in England. Adjoining this corridor is the Assembly Room, probably used by the nuns as a work room, and from there a modern staircase leads to the Sanctum Sanctorum where relics were once preserved; the chest in which St. Bridget's remains were transported home from Rome still rests there.

The monks' quarters lie to the south-west of the church, but the buildings have undergone changes through the centuries. The south wing still dates from the fifteenth century and contains a lovely little Chapter House; the upper floors of the north wing were added in the 1760:ies. To the west of the monks' buildings stands Birgittasystrarnas Vilohem, the present-day rest-home of the Order.

Remains of the foundation walls of other parts of the monastery, which were excavated in the 1920:ies, lie to the west of the church and the buildings here, which separated the nuns' and the monks' quarters, served the needs of visitors and of the mundane economic activities of the monastery.

THE HOUSE OF MÅRTEN SKINNARE

To the north-east of the church across the cemetery stands a strange little red brick building called the House of Mårten Skinnare dating from about 1520. Mårten Nilsson, the Skinner or Furrier, was a pious and immensely wealthy citizen of Stockholm who had been born at Vadstena and where in later life he founded a hospital for the sick, the poor and the weary pilgrims who came to the town. As a Catholic rebel he opposed Gustavus Vasa's Reformation with the result that the king confiscated all his wealth and also his hospital which became joined in 1532 to another institution in the town; from that union the present large mental asylum is descended. After his

156

downfall Mårten was permitted to enjoy the charity of his own foundation at Vadstena for the rest of his life.

The little building—all that is left of the original house—has been partly restored and is notable for its sturdy construction of brick and stone, its bay window, its vaulted rooms, and its niches on the exterior where inmates once sat in the healing sunshine. It is now open to the public but up to recent years it was inhabited by four nurses from the hospital, one of whom would regularly place flowers upon the furrier's grave in the near-by churchyard. That was a gracious gesture which seemed to please the old shade, for according to local lore the nurses would hear him rambling round the house at nights and would sense his benign aura; without the least fear or sense of awe they would speak to him and offer him coffee and cakes.

OTHER VADSTENA BUILDINGS

We can walk back to the quay through the town and on the way we shall pass the brick tower, tall and dominant, which is called, for an obvious reason, the Red Tower. It has stepped gables in a German-Baltic-Gothic style of red brickwork and is all that remains of the town's original parish church built in the early part of the fourteenth century even before the monastery.

South of the Red Tower lies an interesting building called the Bishop's House, one of the oldest surviving private houses in Sweden, built for the Bishop of Linköping in 1473. It served up to the Reformation as the residence of the bishops of Linköping when they visited the monastery at Vadstena.

For those with a special interest, mention must also be made of the old theatre in Vadstena situated off a courtyard lying between the Monastery and the Red Tower. It is one of the oldest provincial theatres in Sweden and remains in the same condition today, with its mythological painted decorations, as when it was built in the 1820:ies.

Taking the westward road of Storgatan we come into a market place on the west side of which stands the Town Hall, dating from about 1400 when the town was founded. Its present appearance was given to it in 1728. From the market place here we can cross a small park to the Castle and so regain our ship just before she sails.

VADSTENA TO BERG

We steam back into the lake, turn north, round Nässjö Point and within an hour we tie up for a few minutes at the canal port of Motala.

MOTALA

The town is best known to the world today as the centre of Swedish broadcasting but it is also a flourishing, modern industrial centre with some 27,000 inhabitants—a strong contrast to the picturesque little medieval town we have just left. Yet this, too, is an ancient settlement and the name means "the place of sacrifice at the meeting of the roads," a hint that a crossing over the Motala Ström has existed here since the dim, pagan past. The building of the canal enlivened the place and at this hamlet, then consisting of no more than a dozen houses and an eighteenth-century church, the headquarters of the Göta Canal Company were established at the start of the enterprise in 1810, and here they remain in the old building that faces the quay.

As we have seen, Platen's dream was to build four new canal towns—at Sjötorp, Lyrestad, Rödesund and Motala—the rest of the Östgöta Line already being well served by Linköping on Lake Roxen and Söderköping to the east. In the end only Motala grew into a town of consequence, though it did not recieve full municipal status until 1881. Platen himself, who has a statue in the market place, laid out the street plan in the form of concentric arcs rising up the hill, and here he established to the east the foundry called Motala Verkstad in which to make the iron goods and ships for the canal. We shall pass these large engineering works on our way to Lake Boren.

The distance along the canal from Motala into Lake Boren is just over two miles, at the end of which, at Borenshult, a dramatic flight of locks carries the canal down into the lake. As the steamer travels along the cut and works through these locks we shall have ample time to walk from Motala along the towpath on the north bank, a pleasant arboreal way. After

ABOVE, *the Göta Canal at Borensberg.*

BELOW, *the headquarters of the Göta Canal Company at Motala.* RIGHT, *the grave of Count Baltzar von Platen (photos by* ERIC DE MARÉ).

The Romanesque Church of the village of Ask in Östergötland, with its wall paintings of about 1500 (photos by ERIC DE MARÉ).

fifteen minutes we reach Platen's resting place beside the water at a spot he chose himself. The grave consists of a huge rough monolith of granite bearing in large gold letters the words "Platens Grav"; an area around it is enclosed with a railing and there lie other grave stones, some to members of Platen's family and one to Gustaf Lagerheim, the young lieutenant we have already mentioned who became chief engineer of the canal.

Soon we reach Motala Verkstad and beyond at Borenshult is the grand staircase of five locks leading down into Lake Boren where a crowd of local people has gathered to watch our ship's locking operations and to wonder about the strange people aboard her. Parallel to the canal to the south Motala Ström has been running and at Borenshult it has dropped 40 feet below the level of the canal; along the river, now dammed, a power station has been built which supplies electricity to the near-by engineering works. If we have remained aboard since leaving Motala, there will be time to step ashore at Borenshult for a bathe at the lakeside establishment at the base of the locks. Then aboard again and across Lake Boren, nearly eight miles long.

LAKE BOREN

We are now in Östergötland and on the Eastern Line of the canal. Already in Lake Boren we can gain an impression of the special character of this part of the waterway. To the right stretches the fertile agricultural plain of the province, its light green fields only occasionally dotted with dark green woodland or a red farmstead. To the left lies a thick forest belt stretching northwards all the way to the provinces of Närke and Söderman-land. The canal divides two types of landscape and sometimes a rocky escarpment on the north stresses the division. This is a rich province, the Well-Favoured Province, of early cultivation and civilization and well-nourished inhabitants of old Gothic stock, tall, fair and Germanic, who proudly declare: "I come from Östergötland, thank God!"

A short way into Lake Boren we pass a promontory on the right, and beyond it can be seen a few stone ruins—all that is left of St. Bridget's home of Ulvåsa to which she first came as a bride of 14 and where she lived for many years. Beyond it, high up on a cliff and enjoying a magnificent view, is a large white house which is the modern manor of Ulvåsa, a grand Palladian building of 1818 still in private ownership.

Out in the lake we can see the distant white towers of three churches; far to the south-west is Ask, to the south-east Ekebyborna and to the north Kristberg. Let us take an imaginary flight across the water to look more closely at these little buildings, for they are typical of the many old churches of Östergötland, and indicate how surprisingly rich Sweden is in old and interesting buildings, considering the comparative poverty, small population, and reliance on timber for building in the past of this once remote northern land.

Ask Church is particularly charming in its rough, unselfconscious, Romanesque way. Though small it has the monumental quality of a miniature cathedral and, like many churches of the district, its inspiration seems to have come from Lund Cathedral with its exceptionally beautiful eastern apse. Ask Church originated in the middle of the twelfth century but the present fabric dates from several periods. Its shingled spire, for instance, is as late as 1745 and most of the windows and the external rendering of the original limestone walls are also eighteenth century. The main plan, however, is the original Romanesque. The simple brick vaulting inside belongs to the fifteenth century and the well-preserved paintings on them, which include some curious little mannikins, are of the same period. The church is unusual in having its tower towards the east and not the west.

Ekebyborna Church lying near the south shore, but further east, is less interesting and complete than Ask but it has a twelfth-century door decorated with some remarkably fine wrought-ironwork and it has an association with St. Bridget, for the tower contains an oratory once used by that great lady.

Kristberg Church on the north shore is mainly of the eighteenth century, including the elaborate shingled roof of the tower, though a church has stood in this spot for 800 years at least. In the south chapel is an unusual, highly formalised Christ on the Cross of medieval workmanship and near the altar stands a quaint carved timber font, brightly painted, in the form of a monk holding a brass bowl on his head, dating from 1678. The most remarkable part of the church, however, is its painted barrel-vaulted ceiling of timber boarding which replaced a stone vault in the 1720:ies. The painting is crude and naïve but vigorous and charming with much florid baroque decorations and some biblical scenes such as Adam and Eve being cast out of Eden.

VERNACULAR PAINTING

The tradition of church painting goes back to medieval times; it was considered valuable not merely decoratively but didactically too in an age when few people could read. Many of the medieval churches in Sweden were of wood and so not many examples remain. One outstanding little timber church has survived since 1323 until today—that at Södra Råda in Värmland. Outside it is plain and simple but all walls and ceilings are covered with brilliant paintings still in perfect state of preservation on their timber background. Those in the choir there are of the same date as the

162

ABOVE, *Södra Råda Church, near Lake Vänern, in the Province of Värmland provides an example of Swedish medieval wall painting.* BELOW, *Risinge Church in the Province of Östergötland offers another example.*

LEFT, *altar relic of peasant craftsmanship of 1701 in Vreta Monastery Church (photo by* ERIC DE MARÉ*).*

ABOVE AND LEFT, *ceiling paintings in Kristberg Church.* RIGHT, *the font of 1678 in the same church (photos by* ERIC DE MARÉ).

*Examples of domestic Swedish
peasant paintings.*

church but those in the nave are later, having been painted by a Swedish monk in 1494.

These church paintings were often executed by local craftsmen, sometimes even by peasants with a gift. For a century between about 1750 and 1850 wall painting was carried into the homes of the peasants themselves to produce a unique folk art. Ever since Viking days decorations with human figures had been made on tapestry and embroidery and this tradition, together with that of mural painting, was applied in the Gothic churches, continued in the baroque palaces and manor houses and brought forth in the gay times of the rococo period this naive, joyful and wholly delightful painting in the homes of the people, which can be called the poor man's gobelins. Some good examples can be seen at the Skansen open-air museum and the Nordic Museum near it at Stockholm.

This painting seems to have been confined mainly to the provinces of Dalarna and Halland, each of which produced a distinct school. In Dalarna the houses were larger and roomier than in other districts and there these frescoes, painted on canvas or thick paper, were fixed permanently on the walls of the parlours of the farmhouses, but in Halland, where life was poorer and the houses smaller, special parlours did not exist so that the paintings there were only hung on special occasions such as Christmas time.

Colouring was always brilliant and subjects were mainly biblical. Dress and architecture were depicted as contemporary and so one may see such scenes as the Queen of Sheba dressed in a crinoline being driven in a stately coach and four. Like all the best phases of creation, this art form had its firm conventions within which the individual artist had plenty of scope for his own fantasies. Cheerful decoration rather than naturalism was the aim; thus when Jesus is depicted preaching in the Temple the sky above may be filled with a giant posy of flowers. There is no attempt at perspective and colouring is so free that a spotted horse may be green and John the Baptist's hair pale blue. Horses, naturally enough among peasants, are popular elements in the compositions, especially in Halland. The Dala paintings are the more familiar and have tended to overshadow those of the Halland school but the Halland paintings are both more amusing and of greater artistry; they are more formalized and are generally shaped in long strips which could be pinned to the low rafters of the dwellings.

This vigorous, vernacular art, which developed to a climax of sophistication, was killed by industrialism and the decline of the old self-sufficient peasant culture. Sixty years ago you could still discover good examples of these paintings lying rolled up in some country attic or decorating the walls of a farmyard closet. Then you could acquire a good piece for a shilling or two but today the paintings are rare and valuable and are eagerly sought by museums and collectors.

BORENSBERG TO BERG LOCKS

At the end of the lake we arrive at Borensberg and descend a shallow regulating lock. This is a small place, important for centuries as a river crossing. The Motala River now flows on the left of the canal and there we can see a fine old granite bridge of low arches built in 1797 and very like the one at Motala. Here are a few small factories, an old timber mill in Falu Red framed in willow trees, and two good hotels—one by the canal also dressed in red and one by the river, a very old inn whose present host deserves a tribute here from the author for having treated him royally and served him with the most tender *chateaubriand* of his life.

The next few miles of the canal are very beautiful in the slanting sunlight, the banks lined with woodland striped by the white boles of silver birches. The river is often glimpsed through the trees to the left until it runs away into the small lake Norrbysjön while we bend southwards for a short stretch towards the pretty little manor of Brunneby and an attendant church with a tall, decorated spire now degraded to a barn. A few miles further on the manor house and then the church of Ljung appear on the left some way off, the manor being approached from a canal bridge up a long and shady avenue.

Ljung Manor is a large, white, somewhat bald, eighteenth-century country mansion of 1774 designed by the rococo architect J. E. Rehn on an axial plan with typical detached side wings. The nearby church, rebuilt in 1808 after a fire, is more distinguished architecturally, being very restrained neo-classical with white stucco walls and a square west tower. Both buildings are interesting in their association with Count Axel von Fersen the Younger (1755—1810) who was born at the manor and was buried in the church. Reputed to be the lover of Marie Antoinette, he organised the abortive attempt of Louis XVI and his family to escape from the French Revolution, but in Swedish history his claim to fame lies in his assassination by an enraged mob when the funeral procession of the Crown Prince Carl August was passing through Stockholm in 1810; without justification, he was suspected of having poisoned the young prince.

The next point of interest is Sweden's Chocolate Town of Ljungsbro, lying between the canal and river to the north—a model industrial village. Out of sight here, down by the river, is the important hydro-electric power station of Malfors, built in 1936 and run entirely by remote control from Motala Power Station.

A LOCK-KEEPER'S LIFE

At Heda we descend the first locks amidst trees. As the sluices are raised and the water pours out of the locks we may wonder what sort of

168

ABOVE, *a tow-path picnic.*
The path runs along the
canal from Motala to
Borenshult. The trees
were planted when the
canal was built. RIGHT,
the locks at Borenshult
(photos by ERIC DE MARÉ*).*

ABOVE, *Vreta Monastery Church (photo by* ERIC DE MARÉ). LEFT, *the garden of Vreta Monastery.*

lives the lock-keepers of the canal may lead. The work seems agreeable enough and apart from occasional hard muscular effort at the lock paddle wheels, it seems an easy life with plenty of time to stand and stare or to cultivate one's garden. And the canal is closed for traffic during the winter months. In spite of all that, a lock-keeper's life is not such a sinecure as it may seem and there is always plenty of work to do. Apart from the routine of helping vessels through the locks all through the long summer days there are many repair and maintenance jobs, such as painting the lock gates, to be carried out. During the winter the lock-keeper (and the bridge-keeper too) may be required to help in canal maintenance such as the repairing of banks or dredging, often far from home. If such occupations do not fill the days the Canal Company can always provide its staff with employment in its forests. The pay is moderate and holidays must be taken in winter. In spite of its idyllic appearance, the lock-keeper's way of life has its disadvantages like every other vocation.

Now we are approaching Berg and on the left bank a simple stone monument can be seen upon which the lettering reveals that it was erected in 1932 to the memory of the 60,000 soldiers and seamen who were employed between 1810 and 1832 in the building of the Göta Canal.

At Berg, quite a small place, the famous, long flight of 11 locks drops us 110 feet down to Lake Roxen, first by a series of two pairs into a wide basin and then by a continuous staircase of seven. Nearly two hours is required for locking down and that allows us time either to bathe in the lake at the *badstrand* at the bottom of the locks, as at Borenshult, or to walk southwards for half-a-mile to inspect the ruins of the medieval convent of Vreta and its beautiful church.

VRETA CONVENT

A Cistercian foundation of 1162, this is one of Sweden's two oldest convents. Only the foundation walls of the convent buildings survive as a flower-filled garden but many parts of the church itself are in their original condition. The tower over the choir with its ogee roof, however, as well as the great main roof of the church were built in 1764 under Carl Johan Cronstedt, a fairly well-known official architect of the rococo period who designed some of the interior decorations at the Stockholm Royal Palace. Some parts of the church are even older than the convent and relics show that a timber church stood here as early as the end of the eleventh century. Until Vadstena was built Vreta was the richest and most important convent in the country.

The building is really two churches in one with a number of projections, mostly in the form of chapels. The lay church to the west has vaulting added in the thirteenth century and to its east is the nuns' church, or choir, with a Greek cross plan. The whole church was admirably restored between 1915 and 1922 and at the same time the foundations of the nunnery were uncovered. As so often happened after the Reformation the buildings of convents and monasteries were allowed to fall into decay, or were used as quarries, while the convent and monastery churches were taken over by the parishes and preserved for the use of the laity. But the foundations of the derelict buildings were not cleared away and so something has been left, as at Vreta, to show us today how medieval monastic life was conducted.

Like Vreta, many medieval stone churches had towers with ornate steeples added to them in the seventeenth and eighteenth centuries, especially during the Golden Age of the baroque. The mixture of styles produces a surprising and interesting harmony of forms, a particularly good example being that of Varnhem Abbey in Västergötland, another Cistercian foundation which Count Magnus Gabriel De la Gardie refurbished about 1650.

Vreta Church also has a baroque addition in the form of an octagonal chapel projecting from the south wall. It is the burial crypt of Field-Marshal Count Robert Douglas and his family, erected in 1663. Robert Douglas (1611-1662) came to Sweden at the age of 17 as one of the thousands of tough, brave Scottish levies who fought under Gustavus Adolphus. Douglas served in the Thirty Years' War and later in Charles X's war with such distinction that he became an honoured man who was ennobled and founded a military family in Sweden. We shall see the ruins of the mighty mansion he built for himself in this locality as we steam across Lake Roxen.

Inside the church the Douglas Chapel should be seen for its copper coffins, marble urns, banners and other panoply. A notable item in the church is the pulpit of carved wood with its white-painted and gilded carvings of saints placed in niches around it—masterly workmanship by an unknown local artist of the mid-seventeenth century. Many other objects of interest are also to be seen—a late eighteenth-century organ, for example, several early medieval tombs, some vigorous baroque wall monuments and a twelfth-century Madonna.

The Monastery Church of Vreta can be visited during the canal journey. It contains many historical monuments including (RIGHT) the chapel of the Douglas family, a grandiloquent relic of 1663, from the period when Sweden was a great power in Europe. Among the members of this noble family here rests the body of Field Marshal Count Robert Douglas, a man of Scottish origin.

ABOVE, *the interior of Vreta Monastery Church.* RIGHT, *Linköping Cathedral.*

Folke Filbyter, the central figure of the Fountain of the Folkunga, by Carl Milles at Linköping.

BERG TO STOCKHOLM

Roxen is large and shallow and the journey across its water to Norsholm is nearly 17 miles. Once out on the lake we can see behind us to the north the stark ruin with its sightless eyes of Robert Douglas's Palace of Stjärnorp which was built in 1654, flourished for a time and then was gutted by fire in 1789. Around the ruin, however, are many unharmed buildings including the original chapel of the castle with its decorated spire and a number of wings and outhouses of the eighteenth century; this is like a village, having a school, a post office and a large farmhouse. Behind the old ruin with its tall tower lies a park, part of which is open to the public, and the tower itself may be entered and climbed for the sake of the fine view over the lake.

To the south-west we can see Kaga Church which, like Ask, is a Romanesque country church. Its spire is late Gothic and within are the remains of some medieval wall paintings.

LINKÖPING

To the south the city of Linköping, the capital of Östergötland, is clearly visible, a great cluster of buildings dominated by the steeple of its famous cathedral. There are, in fact, two Linköpings—the old and the modern. The modern city supports some 69,000 inhabitants and is a rapidly growing industrial centre with many factories, including aircraft works. Old Linköping has pre-Christian roots and in the Middle Ages its importance was surpassed only by that of Uppsala. Here in 1152 the Swedish Church first affirmed its allegiance to Rome.

The cathedral originated about 1150 but it was rebuilt between 1230 and 1550 under influences from France, England and Germany. The spacious interior is remarkably fine, particularly so the east end and the choir. Both outside and inside Linköping is the least disturbed and restored of the Swedish cathedrals, though its tower and steeple, 344 feet high, were added in 1886. Its best feature is the splendid, soaring choir with its apse and three chapels, which replaced a twelfth-century structure in the fifteenth

177

century and is partly the work of masons from western Germany. Good pieces in the interior of the cathedral include a baroque pulpit of 1745 by a Norrköping craftsman, an early fifteenth-century bronze font from Lübeck and an altar-piece of 1542 painted by Maarten van Heemskerck of Holland for the town of Alkmaar in the Nethenlands but acquired by John III for 1200 measures of wheat. The altar-piece contains a figure of Nicodemus bearing the face of Luther.

A notable modern building in Linköping is the Östergötland Museum designed by the architects N. Ahrbom and H. Zimdahl. Completed in 1939 in yellow brick, its two arms enfolding a wide pool over which a willow tree weeps, it is considered to be one of the best provincial museums in the world. Apart from ethnographical and handicraft exhibits, many of local creation, the museum contains a good collection of paintings, including examples by Cranach, Tintoretto and Boucher and by such Swedish masters as Elias Martin and Pehr Hörberg.

Another feature of the town is the romantic fountain erected in the market-place in 1927. Among the best of the works of Carl Milles, it is called the Fountain of the Folkunga and was partly inspired by the novel "Folkungaträdet" by Verner von Heidenstam. The main figure in bronze represents the unprepossessing but heroic old Folke Filbyter on horseback, progenitor of the dynasty of Folkungs, a noble family which was closely associated with Östergötland's medieval history. Around the plinth of the basin are a number of formalised bas-reliefs in granite showing episodes in the Folkunga legend such as Birger Jarl ruling in place of the incompetent King Erik, the Jarl's crusade to Finland and St. Bridget in ecstacy.

Linköping lies on Stångån, the only river in Sweden to run from south to north and a feeder of Lake Roxen. It forms a part of the Kinda Canal.

SÖDERKÖPING

At the east end of Lake Roxen we come to Norsholm which is little more than a communication centre of rail, road and canal but has ancient origins. Here the canal parts company with Motala River which turns northwards towards Lake Glan from where it swings east again to Norrköping and so into the arm of the Baltic called Bråviken.

We steam along through primeval woods, only half sleeping in the bright night and approach one of the pleasing white-painted iron road bridges of the canal which is rolled to one side as we pass through; then down a lock, and soon we enter the long, narrow and beautiful little Lake Asplången. At Snövelstorp we cross the road to Norrköping and see beyond on the right the old tower of Västra Husby Church; then down a lock called Klämman

178

"*Söderköping had a tranquil, unfrenchified, uncaféd, anti-catholic look, that gratified me exceedingly . . .*" (ROBERT COLTON *in "Rambles in Sweden and Gottland," 1847*).
ABOVE, *canal scene from Ramunderberget at Söderköping (photo by* ERIC DE MARÉ*).*

Söderköping Church.
ABOVE, *vaulting.*

BELOW, *the floor monument of Göran Gyllenstierna, one of Gustav Vasa's men, who died in 1575 (photos by* ERIC DE MARÉ).

(the Straits) lying tightly between rocks and, after passing down six more locks, we arrive early in the fresh, bright morning at the old port and spa town of Söderköping.

On the right lie the warehouses on the edge of the town while to the left rises a high granite escarpment which is called Ramunderberget. Up at its top are the remains of the large fort of Ramundersborg built in the sixth century and reputed to have been the home of the legendary giant Ramunder who was some sort of Viking robber with many strange tales attached to his name.

Söderköping was in the Middle Ages the third most important town in Sweden; several Riksdag diets were held here in times past and here Bishop Hans Brask, the last of the Romish supporters before the Reformation and the first proposer of the Göta Canal, set up a printing works; here Birger Jarl was crowned in 1303 and here at one time flourished a large Franciscan monastery. Today Söderköping is an idyllic little town of some 5,500 inhabitants—a small marketing centre relying largely on its spa whose spring has healing properties. Probably the vigorous massage and other treatment given to sufferers who take the cure here is more effective than the water. The quiet spirit of the place with its tree-lined river, its old buildings, its picturesque cobbled streets and pleasant walks in the district around must provide psychic recreation.

Back in medieval times the town was a bustling commercial port, for the river Storå, which runs parallel with the canal into the Baltic at Slätbaken, was then deep and wide enough to allow ships carrying 700 tons to navigate right into the town. In time the river grew smaller and smaller as the land rose on account of a geological process which had been going on ever since the Ice Age; the harbour was moved further and further to the east until it could move no further and the shipping dwindled to nothing. Today the river is only six feet deep and is navigable only by the many small, trim pleasure boats moored along its reedy banks. By the seventeenth century Norrköping was beating its rival and it finally won the maritime and commercial competition in this part of Sweden. Norrköping's population now numbers some 93,000 and the town is a vigorous and uncouth youngster too busy to be concerned any more with the gentle old man of Söderköping dozing in the sun and living on his memories.

However, a new, seasonal and modish life came to the place in the eighteenth century when it became popular as a spa for taking the curative mineral waters of St. Ragnhild's spring. Since then it has been popular among sufferers from rheumatism and such ailments, the more so since 1823 when Dr. Olof Lagberg turned the spa into an effective centre of healing. Today, apart from the local waters, all kinds of baths, electrical and massage treatment, curative gymnastics and so on are provided.

To the name Ragnhild, who gave her name to the healing spring, hangs a legend, which has a number of variations. One of them records that she, a young and lovely nun of the local convent, went forth to pick flowers for the altar and came to the home of the pagan brigand Ramund. The cad attempted to seduce her while she as ardently tried to convert him to Christian beliefs. She returned to the convent after a week wearing a gold bracelet presented to her by Ramund. The holy sisters naturally suspected the worst and she was sent to the stake for having broken her vows of chastity. But Ragnhild was still a virgin and, as the flames rose to consume her, a spring suddenly gushed forth below the pyre and doused the fire. And that, says the legend, was the origin of the healing spring of Söderköping.

The coming of the canal, and then the railway, revived the old town a good deal but even they could not bring back its lost youth. Among its monuments to the past the town contains an eighteenth-century town hall and two old churches—the late thirteenth-century Drothems Church and St. Lars (St. Lawrence) Church built about 1296 on the site of an even older foundation. The latter is the more interesting of the two and is still in an excellent state of preservation. It is an unusual building of red brick-work with curious embellishments of circles, crosses and other shapes of white stucco recessed into its stepped gable ends like blind windows. The character of the building stems from a period of German and Hanseatic domination and is called Baltic Gothic, a style typified by red brickwork, steep gables with stepped tops and church plans having the choir as wide as the rest of the church.

The interior has strong, simple, pointed vaulting of brick inserted about 1400 and also a number of fine possessions which include a crucifix of the same date still hanging in its first position, a splendid north German reredos of about 1500 and an altar painting specially executed for the church by Pehr Hörberg in 1802. Among the monuments is an unusual floor carving in very bold, formalised relief of a recumbent bearded nobleman in armour—Göran Gyllenstierna (died 1575), one of Gustavus Vasa's men.

Just south of the church stands a timber bell tower of 1582 by Anders Börjesson-Stapelmakare (the Tower Builder), the oldest surviving example in this land of timber bell towers, and a magnificent one.

SWEDISH TIMBER BELL TOWERS

These detached timber campaniles of the North were the work of local peasant craftsmen and constituted a special kind of folk art. In the seventeenth century nearly every church in the country had its separate timber bell tower and in spite of the depredations of time and of the Russian

The timber bell tower of 1582 at Söderköping Church.

LEFT, *prehistoric rock carvings in the granite at Himmelstalund near Norrköping.* ABOVE, *the end of the Göta Canal at Mem.*

RIGHT, *a tight squeeze near Mem when an old trading schooner passes a passenger steamer in the narrow cut (photos on this page by* ERIC DE MARÉ).

Stegeborg Castle and the Baltic fjord of Slätbaken.

invaders no less than 450 of these towers still stand. Although the baroque period produced the most varied, most highly developed and most interesting expressions with intricate ogee spires and onion domes, the structural tradition goes back to pagan times. Of the Baltic countries Sweden produced by far the finest flowering of the art.

Some of these Swedish towers were of great height so that their bells could ring out across the lakes and forests to the widely scattered populations. They tend to show regional distinctions in design but two general types are evident—the Open Trestle type and the Enclosed Tower type. Both seem to have been built since early times and often the two are combined in one structure. The example at Söderköping is of the Open Trestle type and is typical in having its great posts protected by tarred shingles of oak like the scales of some reptile; though built in the sixteenth century it is undoubtedly medieval in character.

STEGEBORG CASTLE AND THE BALTIC SEA

A few miles east of Söderköping through rocks, fields and firs we reach the hamlet of Mem where the last lock of the canal lowers us into Slätbaken, a long Baltic fjord, especially lovely on a cloudless summer morning. At the end of it we pass through a narrow sound into wider waters and here on an islet stand the stone ruins of the stronghold of Stegeborg whose tall round tower has been in sight for some time. This was an obvious place for a castle from which to defend the fjord and the port of Söderköping, for the narrow waters on each side of the island could easily be guarded and they could also be piled to prevent the ingress of enemy ships; hence possibly the name Stegeborg or Stäkeborg Stake Fortress. Apart from acting as guardian of Söderköping, Stegeborg Castle was indeed for many centuries the lock and key of all Östergötland.

A stronghold was built here in the early Middle Ages but the remains we see now belong mainly to the mid-fifteenth century; almost nothing remains of the grand fortified palace into which Gustavus Vasa converted the fortress and in which his son, later John III, was born in 1537. John added to, and embellished, the palace and here Charles X passed his childhood. With Charles XI's period of retrenchment and austerity Stegeborg's great days were over; it began to decay and in 1731 it was largely demolished, the stones being used in reconstructing Norrköping which had been almost completely destroyed by the Russian invaders.

To the south of Stegeborg on the mainland can be seen the attractive little church of Skällvik with its charming pointed spire and its detached timber bell tower. The church has very old foundations going back probably to 1100 but it was rebuilt by John III and was thoroughly restored in the early nineteenth century. A notable feature of its interior is a reredos of a painted wood Madonna and Child having side doors with brilliant paintings of St. Bridget, St. Catherine and St. Olof—a rare and beautiful object presumed to be of fifteenth-century, north German workmanship.

Beyond Stegeborg we pass through another sound formed by the island of Eknö, lying to our right, and gradually we emerge through the Östergötland archipelago into the open sea. In the distance to the left lies Arkösund, a small summer resort of the Norrköping people, and within two or three hours we may call in at Oxelösund, originally a fishing hamlet but now an icefree port for the shipping of the iron ore of central Sweden and also a very big industrial centre depending largely on its ironworks. This archipelago journey is a refreshing and stimulating change after the narrower waterways of the lakes and canal and here the steamer can bound along at full speed through salty, open sea between the dark skerries and the swooping seagulls.

A CANAL CAPTAIN'S LIFE

If he is not concentrating his attention on some tricky piece of navigation between the skerries—as at Stendörren (the Stone Door) where the ship must wind in and out on a very snaky course between submerged rocks—we may have a chance to chat with the skipper and to learn something of his life and of the unrecorded lore of his waterway. Let us say we are aboard *Juno* and that the skipper is Vidar Carlsson, a tall, spare man past his middle years and of a simple, kindly disposition. He should know more than most about the waterway for not only has he been employed by the Göta Canal Steamship Company for over 32 years but he began his working days over 50 years ago at the age of 14 as cook and boy aboard his father's sailing vessel which plied regularly along the Göta Canal and in the Baltic Sea carrying all kinds of cargoes—perhaps stone from Gotland to Jönköping or timber from Stockholm to Gothenburg.

Though Captain Carlsson has spent most of his life on the canal he has seen something of the world for he circled the globe in his youth on a Norwegian sailing vessel. His only work ashore was in an ammunition factory in the United States during the First World War but after a year he was at sea again, sailing in the most dangerous war zones. He is still wondering with astonishment how he survived that time. Today he enjoys his peaceful, rhythmical life on the canal as much as he did as an apprentice on his father's schooner. Then sail was the only motive power, apart from the horses and oxen which pulled ships along the narrow cuts, so that a journey between Gothenburg and Stockholm might take as long as three weeks.

188

A shallow lock on the Göta Canal in Östergötland.

The draft animals would be harnessed to a two-wheeled cart in order that the tow-rope could be kept straight and taut. The life was by no means as calm and uneventful as might be expected; the towmen were a rough lot who seem to have had much in common with those "Skufflehunters" who once terrorised the riverside along the upper reaches of the Thames when it was an important commercial navigation. The towmen were often drunk at week-ends and it was then difficult to obtain their services; once persuaded to return to work they would fall asleep as they drove their beasts along and then cart and driver would often tip into the canal.

They would work, say, a six-mile stretch. If the wind was favourable schooners might hoist their sails as they were being towed along and would forge ahead of the animals; then the captain might refuse to pay the driver's full fee and there would be hard words and sometimes hard blows too. Life on the cut is more genteel today, though perhaps less zestful.

It was a good life, declares Captain Carlsson. The work was hard but there was always plenty of good, nourishing food aboard and time for rest and recreation. Life has more problems today, he finds, and one of his immediate problems is to recruit a good crew of boys for his steamer and, once recruited, to keep them—a problem that is becoming more difficult each year because the young men of today can easily find other work and they do not like the long hours on the canal journey nor the hard physical effort.

SÖDERTALJE CANAL

Eventually we turn northwards up Himmerfjärden, the wide sound which separates the mainland from the island of Mörkö. At the north end of this island stands Hörningsholm, a defensive position since the Viking age. Sten Sture the Younger, when fighting the Danes, built an important castle here in the early sixteenth century but it was burned down by the Russians in 1719 and then restored about 1750 by Carl Härleman (1700—53), an outstanding architect, renowned for his homely country houses, who followed Carl Gustaf Tessin as Architect Royal; as already noted, one of his works was the headquarters of the Swedish East India Company in Gothenburg.

Beyond Mörkö we sail up Järnafjärden and then the somewhat narrower Hallsfjärden to reach the two-mile long Södertalje Canal with its large single lock and lofty railway bridge. Södertälje itself is both a modern industrial town and a summer resort, but its origin is lost in the past. It was certainly an important trading centre in Viking times, while in the Middle Ages it rivalled Stockholm as a port. Södertälje did not grow up, as might be thought, as a result of the building of the canal here but was important before that precisely because there was no way through by water and a trans-shipping centre was needed here between lake and sea.

LAKE MÄLAREN

North of Södertälje we pass through Linasundet and steam up Södertäljeviken into Lake Mälaren. Though Sweden's third largest lake after Vänern and Vättern, Mälaren never reveals its true size for it is filled with islands, large and small, and its shores are penetrated by numberless wild bays and inlets. It has its own special character of tree-filled intimacy and around its shores and on its islands stand many signs of early human settlement. Even in Viking times, indeed, this must have been a well-inhabited area because then Mälaren was wide open to the sea both at Södertälje and Stockholm and was a well-protected fjord rather than a lake.

Ahead of us, some four miles away to the north, lies the island of Björkö where once the ancient city of Birka stood—the most important commercial centre of Sweden at the height of the Viking period from where the long ships sailed to the ports of western Europe. Here Ansgar, the Apostle of the North, built the first church in Sweden in the year 830.

We steam round a wide point, turn due east through Bockholmssund and soon we pass Ekerö Church. Five miles further on rises a sheer rock on the left called Kungshatt and there on the top of a pole is an oddity in the form of a huge iron hat. Its origin is obscure but it is said to symbolise the legend of a king who escaped from his pursuing enemies by making his horse jump from the cliff into the lake; in his prodigious leap his hat flew off behind him and so the emblem was erected.

Now we are obviously nearing a great city, for the buildings, beginning with sporadic villas on the rocky islands and shores and an occasional industrial plant, grow thicker and thicker amidst the rocks and the pines until they congeal into large, continuous blocks of bright modern flats. At last the centre of the city comes into sight, framed by the great steel arch of Västerbron which makes a fittingly dramatic watergate to the capital. Beyond the bridge we are in Riddarfjärden and there on the left stands the rich red brickwork of the City Hall above whose tall tower the Three Crowns of gold are sparkling. Everything is glowing with colour in the brilliant evening sunlight as we dock below the Wrangel Palace on the island of Riddarholmen. A crowd of Stockholmers is there to welcome us and on the cobbles the taxicabs are waiting.

RIGHT, *one of the Baltic ports passed on the journey is Oxelösund, originally a fishing hamlet, but now an industrial centre. The town church was erected in 1957 and consecrated to St. Botvid, a local saint. Its tower serves as a sailing-mark.*

190

RIGHT, *"On the Baltic side of Sweden the coast is a mass of small islands, a perfect swarm of them. If you look at them on the map you will see that they look like hundreds of insects fastening on a fruit; they are monotonous enough and very lonely, but they have a landscape of their own as one threads between them in the water always calm, no matter how hard it may be blowing"* (HILAIRE BELLOC in *"Return to the Baltic"*, 1938).

BELOW, *Södertälje Canal has one large, single lock. In 1435 a first attempt was made here to cut a canal between lake and sea, but it was not until 1819 that the connection was achieved. In 1924 the canal was widened.*

STOCKHOLM

To complete this Swedish cross-cut, a rough sketch must be drawn of the capital city and its surroundings, the node of Swedish culture where a seventh part of the country's entire population has concentrated. The sketch cannot be more than an impression to indicate how the place grew through the centuries from a small, defended trading centre to a great modern metropolis—a general map in space and time having a few of its major landmarks outlined.

ITS CHARACTER

Like most clichés, the term Venice of the North is a half-truth. Stockholm is built largely on a group of islands and, though most of them are natural and uncanalised, her waters are ubiquitous. Moreover, the Italian Renaissance has had its influence on the city's buildings, as it has had on nearly every European city. Even the famous City Hall, completed in 1923, has found inspiration in Italy, especially Venice. There Stockholm's similarity to Venice ends.

But Stockholm is certainly a beautiful city as capitals go today. Nature has helped her with rocks and with water, basic elements in pleasing landscape. Islands are everywhere and the city is surrounded by them; to the west Lake Mälaren is filled with them while to the east Saltsjön (Salt Sea) contains an archipelago, or Skärgård, whose islands, islets and skerries extend 80 miles to the north-east into the Baltic. Some 300 years ago Carl X offered 1,000 Crowns to anyone who could count those islands accurately but no one claimed the prize; modern surveyors have numbered them at 10,000.

LEFT, *the tower of Stockholm Town Hall commands a magnificent view over the Old Town.*

195

The beauty of Stockholm is not entirely the product of nature, however; it is also due to an organic but controlled growth and embellishment which has been applied since the town was founded in 1250 by that vigorous ruler of the realm, Birger Jarl. At that time Stockholm was a small settlement and it is possible that it possessed a fort late in the twelfth century. In spite of that fort the place was being continuously harried by pirates and so Birger Jarl at once set to work to make it impregnable with sound fortifications; he realised that it was a good centre for trade and that it was strategically well situated, being easily defended if fortified, being accessible by water for some 75 miles by Mälaren to the west and being in touch by water to the east with the whole of the Baltic.

Here then, where Lake Mälaren pours out its water through Strömmen (the Stream), the shortest river in Europe, into an inlet of the Baltic called Saltsjön, lies the core of the city to which we came at the end of our canal journey. Here at the core are the three islands which form the oldest part of the town—Riddarholmen (Island of Knights), Helgeandsholmen (Isle of the Holy Ghost, where the House of Parliament and the Bank of Sweden now stand) and Staden-mellan-broarna (the Town-between-the-Bridges), the largest of the three which is also called the Old Town and on whose northern end lies the splendid Royal Palace forming the focus of the city.

Of Birger Jarl's original town, all that remains is a considerable part of the street plan in the Old Town and a small part of the defensive town wall, 18 feet thick, which can still be seen in the foundations of the Royal Palace. Stortorget, the Great Market (memorable for its Blood Bath of 1520 when 82 Swedes were slaughtered by the Catholic Danes) is still in its first position.

From the Middle Ages there remain part of Storkyrkan (the Great Church) and Riddarholm Church which began as a Franciscan chapel. Yet the Old Town retains its medieval atmosphere in its narrow, labyrinthine streets which open out here and there into small squares and places and provide fascinating vistas down cobbled passageways to the busy dockside waters.

ITS GROWTH

By the fifteenth century burghers' houses had begun to appear outside the old defensive walls; a few of these still survive, though none in its original form. At this time the stepped gable from Germany and the Low Countries was popular in the north and three examples can still be seen in the Old Town. Some fortifications from the late fifteenth century remain, notably the two round towers on the west of Riddarholmen.

Stockholm did not begin to assume its full position as the national capital until Gustavus Vasa entered the town in state on the Midsummer Eve of

196

The Stockholm Town Hall.

ABOVE, *the Town Hall, designed by Ragnar Östberg, is of handmade brick.* BELOW, *the Göta Canal passengers disembark opposite the Town Hall in the very heart of Stockholm.*

1523 after his victory over the Danes, when the population was a mere 6,000 Then in the seventeenth century Sweden suddenly found herself a powerful country responsible for a whole empire, and so she began to expand her capital as one of the finest in Europe. Many houses from that time still stand in the Old Town with doorways richly carved in the baroque manner. The whole of the quarter west of Stora Nygatan, gutted by fire in 1625, was then rebuilt on a grid-iron plan. Mainly foreign craftsmen were employed in building at that time, especially from Holland, many of whom helped to build two large structures of the period, the two most historical and distinguished monuments in Sweden—the new Royal Palace and Riddarhuset, or the House of the Nobles.

The town continued to expand on the islands and rocks to the north and south of the three central islands. On Södermalm on the south arose Louis De Geer's Palace, designed by a Dutchman, and the old Town Hall designed by the elder Tessin, both of which can still be seen in Götgatan. On Södermalm also arose Katarina Church by Jean de la Vallée which was to be restored later by G. J. Adelcrantz after a fire—the first church in Stockholm to have acquired a dome. To the north, on Norrmalm and Östermalm, the new town plan was in the grand manner of the time with grid-iron street lay-out and axial vistas.

Towards the end of the seventeenth century, Sweden's Golden Age of building, which had lasted for nearly a century, came to sudden end. The Age of Greatness was over and a dull period of retrenchment followed. Things had improved by mid-eighteenth century and another period of cultural brilliance began under the patronage of Gustav III—the age in architecture of Hårleman, Adelcrantz, Carlberg, Cronstedt, Palmstedt and Rehn. Carlberg, for example, largely rebuilt Storkyrkan in the Old Town and gave it a fine new tower; Palmstedt designed the best rococo building in Stockholm—the Exchange in the Great Market; Piper laid out the picturesque park at Haga to the north of the city.

By 1850 Stockholm was still quite a small town with some 100,000 inhabitants. Then industrialism began to affect Sweden and many changes came to the capital expressed in much of the existing building which is in the confused eclecticism of the age and is especially evident on Norrmalm. The railways arrived and other developments too—water and gas on tap, trams, and before long electricity, telephones and bathrooms for all. In the 1860:ies the city fathers planned sensibly with an eye to the future and laid

TOP LEFT, *the Royal Guard is changed in the outer courtyard of the Royal Palace. The parade is an old public ceremony.* BELOW, *the Royal Palace is one of the finest baroque piles in Europe (photo by* ERIC DE MARÉ*).*

199

out Lindhagen's street plan; the results of their foresight can now be seen in the generous, tree-lined avenues of Narvavägen, Valhallavägen, Birger Jarlsgatan, Kungsgatan, Sveavägen, Norr Mälarstrand, Ringvägen on Södermalm, and Strandvägen along the waterside—the latter being one of the better monuments of the Victorian age. Haussmann's Paris plan was obviously the inspiration for this lay-out of broad, straight streets and shady boulevards lined with the façade architecture of bourgeois apartment houses, large and solid.

By 1900 the city's population had trebled to about 300,000 and the suburbs were growing at Lidingö, Djursholm, Sundbyberg and Saltsjöbaden—pleasant middle-class garden cities of widely-separated villas set amidst gardens of rocks and fir trees. During the first two decades of the present century the country grew prosperous and her pride was expressed in that distinctly national style of building with its stress on natural materials, historical antecedents, and fine craftsmanship which reached its apotheosis in Östberg's City Hall.

There followed another great expansion of the capital. Corbusier's creed of Functionalism began to affect the scene—especially after Asplund's brilliant Stockholm Exhibition of 1930. The new flat blocks sprang up everywhere, particularly in the poorer districts of Södermalm—utilitarian structures which were an improvement on the old flat blocks with their dark, central courtyards. The new flats were cramped but they were well fitted and their exteriors were rendered cheerful with bright stuccos and striped sun-blinds, while their severe façades were mitigated by the shapes and shadows of small balconies giving each family its open-air room. The landscaping around these blocks was cheerful too, with sensitive tree planting amidst the rocks and the waters.

The Second World War brought another great expansion, partly on account of the explosive rise in the birth-rate, partly on account of the growing centralization of industry and administration in the capital. Even today the housing problem has not been fully solved, though the satellite centres (like Farsta to the south and Vällingby to the west) now completed or building along the new Tunnelbana (Underground Railway) which runs far to the south and far to the west from the centre, will soon ease the situation. Now the City planners, having completed their work around the capital are reconstructing the central areas, notably near the Concert Hall, off Kungsgatan, where a complex of tall blocks has risen.

RIGHT, *new traffic routes have recently been cut through the old quarters of Stockholm. In the distance are the spires of Riddarholmen Church* (left) *and Clara Church.*

200

ABOVE, *Stortorget (the Great Market) in the Old Town has witnessed many historical events (photo by* JAN MARK).

LEFT, *one of the narrow streets of the Old Town (photo by* ERIC DE MARÉ).

RIGHT, *Västerlånggatan is the main street of the Old Town.*

This wood carving of St. George and the Dragon by Bernt Notke of Lübeck in Stockholm's Great Church is one of the finest examples of medieval sculpture in existence.

ITS PARK SYSTEM

Stockholm's population is now about a million but three things may save her from the final, muddled frenzy of the modern megalopolis. The first is the clean air which keeps all things fresh in appearance. The second is the remarkable system of inter-penetrating parks and public gardens which, combined with the water and contrasting with the closely built-up areas, bring nature into the centre of the town, provide interesting pictures wherever you look and give a sense of spaciousness. The third is the water and the close contact it gives with the surrounding countryside which eases the sense of being trapped within walls that is so pressing in most large towns. Indeed, part of the city's charm is certainly due to the little passenger steamers, immaculately white, which lie moored in rows along the many quays or go puffing proudly out to some settlement among the skerries.

The municipality has in the past acquired much of the land in and around Stockholm and has thus been able to reserve considerable areas as parks and open spaces. It has linked these up with the old parks and gardens to form a whole system. Of the old parks there is the eighteenth-century Haga Park to the north, Kungsträdgården at the centre which was a royal garden as early as the fifteenth century, and Humlegården (Hop Garden) near the centre which Gustav Adolph laid out in 1619. The chief fascination of the Stockholm park system is its intimate informality and there the old English tradition of the picturesque has had its effect as well as oriental influences brought with the eastern trade in the eighteenth century. The mile-long strip park lying between the high flat blocks and Lake Mälaren along Norr Mälarstrand on Kungsholmen is typical of the style. With this charming public gardening goes a high level of design in street furniture—of brightly painted litter bins, kiosks, seats, lamp-standards, railings and, last but not least, those famous concrete pots brimming over with flowers which have set a European fashion.

Not many of the parks are very large excepting the two on the outskirts—Haga to the north and Djurgården to the east. The latter is the Richmond Park of Stockholm and it was, indeed, a royal deer park at one time. It is now a public resort for walking and riding and is not unlike Richmond Park in appearance, being planted with oak trees in an informal English manner.

OLD BUILDINGS OF NOTE

Dominating the Old Town right at the centre of the city is:—

The Royal Palace, which is one of the finest baroque piles in Europe—baroque at its most dignified and serene. Its building came about in the following way. The old Palace, partly medieval, had become delapidated by

Christina's time and so the Queen decided to rebuild it. But she abdicated and it was left to her cousin Charles X to give the order to Jean de la Vallée to prepare drawings. These were ready in 1656 and the work had hardly begun when the king died. Later the elder Tessin prepared a design but it was not until 1688 that his son began to develop the plans which were to be finally realized.

Nicodemus Tessin the Younger (1654—1728) was Sweden's Christopher Wren. He succeeded his father as Architect Royal and lived to become not only the country's most famous architect but university chancellor, State Councellor, Lord High Chamberlain and Earl as well. He was a doctrinaire classicist and turned always to France or Italy for inspiration; he was, indeed, a pupil of Bernini in Rome for a time.

The whole of the north block was finished in 1694, the side wings being added during the next three years. In 1697 a fire destroyed the remaining old palace but luckily the new works were saved. In 1728 Tessin died and his son Carl Gustav took over the work. Owing to the changed conditions of the time progress was slow and the whole edifice as we now see it with its huge inner quadrangle was not completed until 1754. It had been begun as the grand residence of an absolute monarch ruling a powerful state; it was completed for a constitutional monarch of a small country which had lost an empire. Yet it is the grandest, the most unified and the most beautiful of Europe's royal palaces. Perfectly sited above the water with its noble axial approach from Gustavus Adolphus' Market on Norrmalm, by way of Adelcrantz's granite bridge of 1806, its simple, bold massing, its strong stone base supporting the long façades of buff stucco (originally yellow), its stone dressings, its rhythmical windows, its entrances like triumphal arches decorated with sudden, vigorous carving, it represents classical architecture at its most highly developed and assured.

The State rooms of the Palace are open to the public at certain times and here can be seen, amidst the usual royal bric-à-brac, many fine objects and several fine interiors. The royal collection of tapestries is renowned and in the Palace a number of examples from the collection can be seen— Flemish, Beauvais and Delft.

Riddarhuset, the parliamentary House of Nobles, is the second of Stockholm's finest old buildings. It stands a few minutes walk from the Palace on the northwest corner of the Old Town—an architectural landmark of the seventeenth century built of red brick with ogee copper roof, sandstone Corinthian pilasters and other dressings. Its character is distinctly Dutch Renaissance and it was, in fact, initiated by a gifted French architect, Simon de la Vallée, who had worked in Holland, and a Dutch architect, Joost Vingbooms, continued it in 1656. Jean de la Vallée, a son of Simon, finished the job by 1674. In this admired building, with its great hall decorated

206

ABOVE, *the statue of King Gustav III with the National Museum in the background across the bay.* BELOW, *the Bank of Sweden and the House of Parliament behind it, with the Royal Palace to the right.*

The city planners, having completed their work around the capital, are now reconstructing the central areas. A complex of tall blocks with a pedestrian precinct has arisen near the Concert Hall.

Slussen, the Lock, connecting Lake Mälar with the Baltic Sea, was formerly crossed by a little drawbridge. Now a clover-leaf crossing with a maze of bridges and tunnels has taken its place.

*Stockholm of today has 111 districts and is sur-
rounded by planned suburbs. Among them are
Vällingby* (ABOVE, LEFT)*, Skönstaholm* (ABOVE)
and Farsta (BELOW)*.*

with a ceiling painting by Ehrenstrahl, the nobles met for political discussion right up to the reconstitution of 1866.

The Palace of Karlberg, completed in 1670 and the third most important seventeenth-century monument in Stockholm, was also designed by Jean de la Vallée who became a naturalised Swede and was largely patronised by Queen Christina's Chancellor, Count Magnus Gabriel De la Gardie, a great and extravagant builder. With its central courtyard, its tiered roof and top rows of bold, circular windows decorated with swags, it is a strong and unusual building. It lies outside the town to the north-west, having been a hunting lodge at one time. It became a military academy in the eighteenth century and is still one today. The low side wings were added by the architect C. C. Gjörwell in 1795, though the stables are the work of Carl Hårleman and date from 1736. North of the palace lies a very pleasant public park filled with trees and containing a little Temple of Neptune also designed by Gjörwell.

Many other old houses and palaces are to be seen in or around Stockholm. Only one will be mentioned in this brief survey—the delightful King's Pavilion in Haga Park, a little royal retreat of 1792 still containing its contemporary interiors. It is open to the public and the Mirror Hall and the Pompeian Hall are particularly worth inspection.

OLD CHURCHES

Back in the Old Town we must take a quick look at three notable old churches. Like most old churches none was built all at one time and all are history books in stone and brick.

Storkyrkan, the Great Church or the Church of St. Nicolaus, is the city's cathedral and the oldest church in Stockholm, at least in parts for it was almost entirely rebuilt about 1740 by Carlberg. In spite of that reconstruction no less than 13 periods of building during five centuries can be discovered here. The church was founded by Birger Jarl in the 1260:ies but only inside has any part of the Gothic fabric survived. From its pulpit in 1525 Olaus Petri, the Swedish Luther who superintended the translation of the Bible into Swedish, sang mass for the first time in the Swedish language and so inaugurated the Reformation in the country. He lies buried here beneath the pulpit.

Storkyrkan contains two interesting antiques. The first is the large wooden statue of St. George and the Dragon executed by the Lübeck sculptor Bernt Notke and presented to the church in 1489 by Sten Sture the Elder in memory of the Battle of Brunkeberg of 1471 when the Danes under Christian I were defeated. It is one of the finest pieces of medieval sculpture in existence. The second antique is the strange painting called *Väder-*

211

solstavlan (Picture of the Mock Suns), painted in 1535 by order of Petri to commemorate an extraordinary celestial phenomenon observed over Stockholm in that year—five mock suns encircled by coronas. As an astronomical record the picture is interesting, but it is equally interesting as a record of how the city looked over four centuries ago.

Riddarholm Church may be called Sweden's Westminster Abbey in that it contains the remains of many Swedish kings and famous men. It is now solely a mausoleum and is not used for worship any more. It was built at the end of the thirteenth century as a Franciscan abbey church and a considerable part of the original structure remains; the south transept, however, is late sixteenth century and most of the burial chapels are seventeenth century. Of these chapels the most noteworthy is that of Gustavus Adolphus which was built in Dutch style in 1634. The finest addition is the attached Carolinean Chapel north of the choir which was built between 1671 and 1743 to contain the remains of the tenth, eleventh and twelfth of the Charles; the elder Tessin and Hårleman were the designers. Within the church are some early frescoes, an altar-piece by the younger Tessin and a fine silver chandelier made in Augsburg in the early seventeenth century. The spire of the building was burned down in 1835 and replaced by a peculiar black affair of open cast-ironwork designed by the sculptor E. G. Göthe.

The German Church, or Tyska Kyrkan, was built for the German community between 1613 and 1618. Most of the original structure still stands but the tower was rebuilt in 1886 after a fire. The interior, with its elaborate altar-piece, is a good, unspoiled example of the mid-seventeenth century.

MUSEUMS AND ART GALLERIES

The National Museum is on the south-east tip of Norrmalm where the bridge crosses to Skeppsholmen—an ugly building of 1866 containing the most interesting and valuable art collection in the country. The founder of the collection was that great patron of the arts, Gustav III, who bought for the State the many works of art acquired by Carl Gustaf Tessin when he was ambassador in France. To this the King added his own private collection. The museum is especially noted for its eighteenth-century paintings, including many Flemish and Dutch works, but it also contains magnificent furniture, porcelain, clocks, silverware, glassware and textiles of different periods and from various lands; also a large collection of drawings and engravings, only a small number of which can, of course, be displayed.

The National Historical Museum (Statens Historiska Museum), in Östermalm, was founded in 1786 on the basis of a collection of antiques made

212

One of the newest sky-scrapers of Stockholm is Wenner-Gren Center. It houses scientists from different parts of the world.

ABOVE, *the Mora farmstead of the sixteenth century from Dalarna at Skansen, Stockholm's open-air folk museum (photo by* ERIC DE MARÉ*).*

LEFT, *Skansen has a zoological section (photo by* JAN MARK*).*

TOP RIGHT, *the small timber church of Seglora, now at Skansen.* BELOW RIGHT, *the Skogaholm manor house, brought to Skansen from the vicinity of Örebro.*

by Gustavus Adolphus. It now contains a prehistoric and medieval collection and an excellent library. Here also is a royal collection of coins.

The Nordic Museum, at the north-west corner of the island of Djurgården to the east of the city and approached by Strandvägen, owes its origin largely to the efforts of Dr. Artur Hazelius, a teacher of languages, who in 1872 began to make a collection of objects illustrating Swedish culture of the past. Now the museum contains examples of Swedish arts and crafts from the Middle Ages down to the present day. Of special interest here is the collection of a type of folk art which is exclusive to Sweden—the wall paintings which decorated the peasant dwellings between the years 1750 and 1850 mainly in the provinces of Dalarna and Halland.

Skansen, meaning a small fort or redoubt, is the outdoor extension of the National Museum and is, of course, world-famous as the first of the Scandinavian open-air museums of national culture, having been founded by Hazelius in 1891.

Occupying the high ground on the west of Djurgården and approached either by steps or by escalator, it is a park as well as a museum. Amidst the indigenous trees stand many old buildings—peasant farmsteads and cottages from different provinces and periods, manor houses, bell towers, windmills, an old timber church, a Lapp encampment and so on. There is also a zoological section containing live animals of the North as well as restaurants, a belvedere, dwellings of famous people, a typical Swedish market place, an open air theatre, a dance floor, a band stand and an old town quarter where traditional crafts such as glassblowing are demonstrated. It is a fascinating place and should not be missed by visitors to Stockholm.

The Biological Museum stands near the entrance to Skansen and here can be seen a good collection of Scandinavian birds and animals. Other specialist museums are:—

The Maritime Museum, the Technical Museum and *the Ethnographical Museum* all lying close together on the mainland north of Djurgården beyond the Diplomats' Town. *The Museum of Natural History* lies to the north-west of Stockholm in the Frescati district. *The Royal Army Museum* is housed in a building of 1770 by Cronstedt in the Östermalm district. *The Stockholm City Museum* is at No. 1 Götgatan on Södermalm, formerly Stockholm's Town Hall, a building by the elder Tessin, wherein are many interesting items relating to Stockholm's history through the centuries. *The Postal Museum* in the Old Town contains a good stamp collection and

LEFT, *Millesgården on Lidingö (a suburban island of Stockholm) was presented to the public at his death by Carl Milles, the sculptor, and contains a number of his works in a garden setting.*

illustrations of postal carriage from early times. *The Egyptian Museum,* also in the Old Town, is housed in the ground floor of Lotsstyrelsen (Pilot Board) House, a building of 1680 which the elder Tessin designed for the National Bank; the collection contains rare finds from ancient Egypt.

MODERN ARCHITECTURE

Swedish twentieth-century architecture is world-famous and has had a profound influence throughout Europe. It is possible that the visitor to Stockholm will be more interested in, and more impressed by, her contemporary buildings than by her old ones. The new schools are particularly good, for the children in Sweden form a privileged class. Paul Hedqvist's Southern Communal School and his Technical School are fine examples. The structures of the new underground railway system, though austere, rise far above mere utilitarianism to a high architectural level.

Tengbom's City Concert Hall with its attenuated Corinthian portico columns, Asplund's City Library with its great rotunda, Asplund's moving Crematorium in the South Cemetery are notable buildings. But the most famous building of the century in Stockholm is the City Hall by Ragnar Östberg which rises on a perfect site on the south-east corner of Kungsholmen facing the waters of Riddarfjärden, the eastern end of Lake Mälaren. The drawings for the City Hall were first made in 1909 but the building was not finished until 1923. In its creation all the leading artists and craftsmen in Sweden were co-opted to give their best and the final cost was over £ 1 million. Though modern in feeling, this *tour-de-force* is not modern in the sense of being cubistic or functionally utilitarian, or in using revolutionary building techniques and new materials. With its dark-red, hand-made brickwork, its courtyard plan, its tall, elegant tower surmounted by a copper lantern and a gilded roof, its careful detailing, its lovely carillon, its many ornaments of sculpture, painting and mosaics, its textural richness and colour, the building is an example of the swan-song of handicrafts—and of revived handicrafts at that. Though eclectic in conception it could not have been designed at any other time in history or in any other country. It is a fantasy, a fairy-tale, brilliantly told. Even if one regards it as a piece of theatrical scenery, it is impossible to assess the Stockholm City Hall as anything but a masterpiece of its kind.

RIGHT, *Drottningholm Palace dates from the late seventeenth century. It was inspired by Versailles and has a rococo garden. It is a residence of the King of Sweden, but parts of it are open to the public, including its remarkable eighteenth-century theatre* (RIGHT BELOW).

EXCURSIONS FROM STOCKHOLM

Many excursions from the city can be made by boat, train, bus or car, either into the archipelago or into Lake Mälaren or up to the University and Cathedral City of Uppsala. Between Stockholm and Uppsala lies the ancient and idyllic little town of Sigtuna with its Romanesque ruins and its eighteenth-century courthouse, while between Uppsala and Sigtuna, the great seventeenth-century manor house, or "castle" of Skokloster, with its many treasures, stands four-square by Mälar's shore. Here only two of the more popular and interesting excursions by steamer will be described—to Drottningholm and to Gripsholm.

Drottningholm Palace, sometimes called Sweden's Versailles, is the royal summer residence, though most of the rooms are open to the public. The park and the outbuildings are not the least interesting features of the whole place. It lies some ten miles to the west of Stockholm and can be reached by road, rail or steamer the last form of transport being the most attractive if time is not pressing. The steamer leaves Klarastrand near the City Hall at regular times and the journey takes about 50 minutes.

The present building followed an earlier one destroyed by fire in 1661 and it was begun in the following year for the Dowager Queen Hedvig Eleonora, widow of Charles X, the architect being Tessin the Elder. It is that architect's greatest work and is an imposing baroque monument of stone and stucco in a French style planned with rigid symmetry amidst formal gardens in the style of Le Nôtre. The symmetry, typical of the grand theatricality of those times of royal and aristocratic power, is so strained that of the two domes at the extremities of the building, one covers a chapel and the other a kitchen.

The building was continued by the younger Tessin and the whole, with its terrace and formal gardens, was completed by 1700 except for the low side

LEFT, *the post-Reformation castle of Gripsholm on Lake Mälar can be reached by boat from Stockholm.*

wings by Hårleman which were added 40 years later. The palace was much favoured by Gustav III and here in his time court life was brilliant and gay. Inside the palace is a grand central staircase and around it lie many over-crowded rooms, some decorated with paintings by Ehrenstrahl. Louise Ulrica's library conceived by that clever draughtsman and designer of the rococo period, the genial Jean Eric Rehn (1717—93), is a particularly handsome room and the Mortlake tapestries of the seventeenth century in the Oscar Salon should not be missed.

In the French gardens stand some excellent bronze statues by Adrian de Fries which were captured at Prague in 1648, while on the grand axis stands Fries's great Neptune Fountain of bronze made for Christian IV of Denmark and captured by the Swedes as booty from Frederiksborg Castle in Denmark in 1659.

Near the Palace to the north lies the fascinating Court Theatre designed by C. F. Adelcrantz for Gustavus III in which the king loved to indulge his passion for drama. The theatre is still in full working order exactly as it was when first erected.

Beyond the formal French gardens to the west is the informal English park laid out by F. M. Piper in the eighteenth century and there, to the south-west, will be found the rococo Chinese Pavilion of the 1760:ies which is also the work of Adelcrantz, though decorated internally by Rehn. This little structure is perhaps the most charming example of Chinoiserie in Europe. It was first transported in sections by water from Stockholm like a modern prefabricated house and erected in the park here as a surprise birthday present from King Adolph Frederick to his wife, Louise Ulrica, sister of Frederick the Great of Prussia. The birthday occasion was a festive one; the whole court dressed up in Chinese costumes, among those present being the seven-year-old Crown Prince who was later to be crowned Gustavus III.

Before returning to Stockholm we can refresh ourselves at the excellent restaurant, housed in an eighteenth-century manor house near the landing stage.

Gripsholm Castle is the objective of the second of our suggested excursions and this can also be reached by the waters of Mälaren. The steamer leaves Klara Strand, Stockholm, several times a week and takes three hours to reach Gripsholm which stands about a half-mile from the small, medieval town of Mariefred on the southern shore of Lake Mälaren. The small town itself is worth visiting for the sake of its local museum, seventeenth-century church, and enchanting classic courthouse of timber.

This romantic and picturesque building with its informal grouping of cylindrical towers set amidst woods and water is quite different from Drottningholm, being one of Gustavus Vasa's defensive palaces of the Re-

The Palace of Karlberg, completed in 1670, was designed by Jean de la Vallée. It is a strong and unusual building in baroque style, which now houses a military academy (photo by ERIC DE MARÉ).

ABOVE, *the Cathedral of Uppsala, the biggest church in Sweden.*

LEFT, *the castle of Skokloster on Lake Mälar, completed in 1658, is another place which can be reached by boat from Stockholm. The founder, Field Marshal Carl Gustaf Wrangel, did not live to see his work completed.* TOP LEFT, *the Royal Saloon with paintings of three Carolean kings.* BELOW LEFT, *the main Entrance Hall.*

formation retaining a certain medieval air. It is of ancient foundation, for Chancellor Bo Jonsson erected a fortification here in the 1380:ies and it is from his crest of a griffin that the name Grip is derived. His castle was destroyed during the rising under Engelbrekt in 1434; then Sten Sture the Elder rebuilt it and in 1498 presented the property to the monastery he had founded at Mariefred. In 1537 Gustavus Vasa appropriated it when he dissolved the monasteries and built the existing structure to the plans of von Cöllen, a German architect. Additions have been made by his successors, including Gustavus III who held his scintillating court here and erected the small theatre for its entertainment among other new amenities.

Now the place belongs to the State and is open to the public as a museum noted for its collection of portraits of royal and famous people of different periods. The castle has many fine rooms including the Great Hall of State and the Duke Charles's Chamber, the only one to retain its decorations from the Vasa age; a number of smaller rooms are decorated in the Gustavian style of the eighteenth century. There is a garden by the lake laid out in 1727 by Hårleman and a deer park stretches away to the west of the castle.

So back to town, perhaps to dine and wine at the Opera House restaurant, or at Konstnärshuset (the Artists' House), or at Berns maybe, that old Bohemian haunt and nostalgic relic of the nineteenth-century Restaurant Cult, or perhaps up on the hill-with-a-view at Skansen. Wherever you go the schnapps will be stimulating, the food will be good and the glittering waters will encompass you in the exotic northern twilight.

THE END

LEFT, *Uppsala, which is soon reached from Stockholm, is one of Sweden's oldest cities, founded in the thirteenth century. The University, the oldest in Sweden, was founded in 1477. The castle of Uppsala was begun in 1545 by King Gustav Vasa.*

LEFT, *the passenger steamer Diana on the Göta Canal.*—ABOVE, *locking down near Mem (photo by* ERIC DE MARÉ*).*

229

ACKNOWLEDGEMENTS

The author sincerely thanks the many kind Swedish people who have helped him so generously in making this book, notably members of the Swedish Institute for Cultural Relations (Svenska institutet för kulturellt utbyte med utlandet), the Swedish Travel Association (Svenska Turisttrafikförbundet), the Göta Canal Company (Göta Kanalbolag, Motala), and the Göta Canal Steamship Company (Rederi AB Göta Kanal). Special thanks go to Dr. Gunnar Ahlström of the Swedish Institute for his personal encouragement and general advice, to Fröken Ulla Fägerskiöld of the Swedish Travel Association for checking the facts about the canal journey, to Rektor Herbert Lundh of Uppsala University for checking the history of the Göta Canal, to Direktör Gösta Hallin of the Göta Canal Company for checking facts in the text and to Direktör K.-Å. Johansson of the Göta Canal Steamship Company for checking time-tables etc and for helping with illustrations and maps.

If otherwise not mentioned the photographs in this book were taken by Erik Liljeroth, Allhem Publishing House.

ERIC DE MARÉ

Medallion designed by Erik Lindberg in 1922
to celebrate the centenary of the Göta Canal.

TABLE OF MONARCHS

St. Erik

Olov Skötkonung. About 1000
Anund Jakob. About 1020-1050
Emund Gamle. About 1050-1060

THE DYNASTY OF STENKIL

Stenkil. About 1060-1066
Halsten and Inge the Elder. About 1080-1110
Filip and Inge the Younger. About 1110-1122
Ragnvald Knaphövde. Dead about 1130

THE DYNASTIES OF SVERKER AND ERIK

Sverker the Elder. About 1130-1156
Erik IX (St. Erik). About 1156-1160
Karl (VII) Sverkersson 1161-1167
Knut Eriksson 1167-1196
Sverker the Younger 1196-1208
Erik (X) Knutsson 1208-1216
Johan (I) Sverkersson 1216—1222
Erik (XI) Eriksson 1222-1229 and 1234-1250
Knut Långe 1229-1234

Karl Knutsson (Bonde)

THE DYNASTY OF THE FOLKUNGS

Birger Jarl. Regency 1250-1266
Valdemar 1250-1275
Magnus Ladulås 1275-1290
Torgils Knutsson. Regency 1290-1298
Birger Magnusson 1290-1318
Magnus Eriksson 1319-1365
Erik (XII) 1357-1359
Håkan 1362-1371
Albrekt of Mecklenburg 1363-1389

Gustav Vasa

UNION AND HOME RULERS

Margareta. Regent 1389-1412
Erik (XIII) of Pomerania. 1396-1439
Engelbrekt. Regent 1435-1436
Karl Knutsson Bonde. Regent 1436-1440
Kristofer 1440-1448
Karl (VIII) Knutsson. 1448-1457, 1464-65 and 1467-70
Christian (I) 1457-1464
Sten Sture the Elder. Regent 1470-1497 and 1501-1503
Hans (Johan II) 1497-1501
Svante Sture. Regent 1504-1512
Sten Sture the Younger. Regent 1512-1520
Christian (II) 1520-1521

Erik XIV

Gustav II Adolf

Queen Kristina

THE DYNASTY OF THE VASAS

Gustav I Vasa. Regent 1521-1523. King 1523-1560
Erik XIV 1560-1568
Johan III 1568-1592
Sigismund 1592-1599
Karl IX 1599-1611
Gustav II Adolf 1611-1632
Kristina 1632-1644

THE DYNASTY OF PFALZ

Karl X Gustav 1654-1660
Karl XI 1660-1672
Karl XII 1697-1718
Ulrika Eleonora 1718-20
Fredrik I of Hessen 1720-1751

Karl XI

THE DYNASTY OF HOLSTEIN-GOTTORP

Adolf Fredrik 1751-1771
Gustav III 1771-1792
Gustav IV Adolf 1792-1809
Karl XIII 1809-1818

THE DYNASTY OF BERNADOTTE

Karl XIV Johan (Bernadotte) 1818-1844
Oscar I 1844-1859
Karl XV 1859-1872
Oscar II 1872-1907
Gustav V 1907-1950
Gustaf VI Adolf 1950-

Karl XII

Gustav III

Karl XIV Johan

Gustav V

Gustaf VI Adolf

The passenger steamer Vadstena entering Vadstena harbour. In the foreground lies an old dredger. Oil painting of 1860 by Emerentia Sjöholm in the Östergötland Museum.

INDEX

An asterisk (*) after a figure denotes an illustration; a figure in italics denotes that the object is mentioned in a caption; (f.) denotes "and the following page," (ff.) denotes "and the following pages."

234

235

Reverse of medallion designed by Erik Lindberg in 1922.
The obverse of the medallion is shown on page 230.

Printed in Sweden

AB ALLHEMS TRYCKERIER
MALMÖ 1964